PRACTICE
MAKES
PERFECT®

Basic Japanese

Premium Third Edition

Eriko Sato, PhD

Mc
Graw
Hill

New York Chicago San Francisco Athens London Madrid
Mexico City Milan New Delhi Singapore Sydney Toronto

Acknowledgment

The author greatly appreciates the useful suggestions provided by Ms. Carolyn Laurino at Stony Brook University and the kindest professional help provided by Mr. Christopher Brown at McGraw Hill.

1   2   3   4   5   6   7   8   9   LHS   28   27   26   25   24   23

ISBN   978-1-265-10026-1
MHID   1-265-10026-8

e-ISBN   978-1-265-10602-7
e-MHID   1-265-10602-9

McGraw Hill, the McGraw Hill logo, Practice Makes Perfect, and related trade dress are trademarks or registered trademarks of McGraw Hill and/or its affiliates in the United States and other countries and may not be used without written permission. All other trademarks are the property of their respective owners. McGraw Hill is not associated with any product or vendor mentioned in this book.

McGraw Hill products are available at special quantity discounts to use as premiums and sales promotions or for use in corporate training programs. To contact a representative, please visit the Contact Us pages at www.mhprofessional.com.

McGraw Hill is committed to making our products accessible to all learners. To learn more about the available support and accommodations we offer, please contact us at accessibility@mheducation.com. We also participate in the Access Text Network (www.accesstext.org), and ATN members may submit requests through ATN.

McGraw Hill Language Lab App
Audio recordings are available to support your study of this book. Go to www. mhlanguagelab.com to access the online version of this application. A free mobile version is available in the iOS app store (for iPhones and iPad) and the Google Play store (for Android phones). See inside cover for more details.

Contents

Introduction

Practice Makes Perfect: Basic Japanese is designed as a study tool for beginning students of Japanese or as a review for intermediate students of Japanese. It can serve as a helpful self-study tool or as supplementary material for high school or college students of Japanese. It starts with the basic sound and writing systems and provides useful vocabulary and basic grammar so you can communicate in authentic Japanese. You'll learn how to meet new people, hold short conversations, make suggestions, make requests, and express ideas by comparing and contrasting.

Chapters are organized in such a way that learners can understand the characteristics of each building block of Japanese sentences and then gradually gain insight into how these building blocks are combined and used with a variety of vocabulary words for a variety of authentic communicative functions.

Each chapter includes a number of short units, each of which focuses on a single functional, situational, or grammatical concept, such as "Entering your friend's house with おじゃまします **ojamashimasu**" and "Expressing desire with ...たい **tai**." Each unit can be completed in 20–30 minutes and provides the concise usage or grammar explanation needed for the purpose of the unit, as well as a thematically collected list of vocabulary, such as words for describing personality. Examples are written in authentic Japanese script and are accompanied by Romanization to clarify the ambiguity in the pronunciation of **kanji** (Chinese characters) and word boundaries as well as to accommodate those who have not gained full command in using the Japanese scripts. Each example is also followed by an English translation to help users learn new vocabulary and sentence structure.

Exercises are carefully presented so that they can mostly be done using the vocabulary words provided in the same unit or in the preceding units; short glossaries are occasionally provided in parentheses wherever they may be needed. Exercises vary: Some are sentence or dialog completion questions, others are reading comprehension questions, and still others are open-ended questions that encourage learners to express themselves freely, using the vocabulary and grammar/usage knowledge they acquired in the unit and the help of a dictionary.

Learning another language requires dedication, time, and frequent practice. By using *Practice Makes Perfect: Basic Japanese*, students at any level can gain or clarify how to use words and structures and strengthen their expressive power in the Japanese language through practice. Only practice makes perfect.

Let's say and write Japanese words!

This chapter introduces the Japanese sounds as well as basic Japanese writing systems. The Japanese sounds are very easy to pronounce except for a few consonants and syllables. By contrast, the Japanese writing system is quite complex. A Japanese sentence can be written by combining two phonetic systems, called **hiragana** and **katakana**, as well as Chinese characters adapted to Japanese, called **kanji**. You will learn how to correctly read and write each **kana** character. You will also see examples of how to use kanji characters.

Basic Japanese sounds and kana characters

There are 46 basic hiragana characters and an equivalent 46 basic katakana characters, each of which represents a syllable sound. Hiragana is used to represent grammatical items and content words that are not written in kanji or katakana. Katakana is used to represent non-Chinese foreign proper names and words from non-Chinese foreign cultures. (Chinese names and things from Chinese culture can be written in kanji.) Katakana can also be used to represent sound symbolisms and items in Japanese pop culture.

As you will learn later in this chapter, the same usage conventions, such as diacritics and small-sized characters, apply to both hiragana and katakana. However, there is one exception: The long vowels are represented by the elongation mark (ー) in the katakana system but not in the hiragana system.

The following table lists the basic kana characters; in this table, each cell contains a hiragana character, a katakana character, and the Romanization (**romaji**), from left to right.

あ ア a	い イ i	う ウ u	え エ e	お オ o
か カ ka	き キ ki	く ク ku	け ケ ke	こ コ ko
さ サ sa	し シ shi	す ス su	せ セ se	そ ソ so
た タ ta	ち チ chi	つ ツ tsu	て テ te	と ト to
な ナ na	に ニ ni	ぬ ヌ nu	ね ネ ne	の ノ no
は ハ ha	ひ ヒ hi	ふ フ fu	へ ヘ he	ほ ホ ho
ま マ ma	み ミ mi	む ム mu	め メ me	も モ mo
や ヤ ya	------	ゆ ユ yu	------	よ ヨ yo
ら ラ ra	り リ ri	る ル ru	れ レ re	ろ ロ ro
わ ワ wa	------	------	------	を ヲ o (wo)
ん n	------	------	------	------

Japanese has five basic vowels:

- **a,** which sounds like the first vowel in *father*
- **i,** which sounds like the vowel in *eat*
- **u,** which sounds like the vowel in *boot,* but without lip rounding
- **e,** which sounds like the vowel in *egg*
- **o,** which sounds like the vowel in *oat*

The vowels are reprented by the characters in the first row in the preceding table. Note that the consonants **r** and **f** are quite different in Japanese than in English:

- Japanese **r** is made by tapping the tip of the tongue behind the upper teeth just once, like the brief flap sound *tt* in *letter* in American English. As shown in the above table, **r** is represented in five different basic hiragana or katakana characters.
- The characters ふ and フ are specified as **fu** but are pronounced by bringing the upper and lower lips close to each other and blowing air between them gently.

Additional sounds can also be represented, using a single character combined with diacritics or using two characters, as discussed later in this chapter. For now, you just need to know that pitch can contribute to word meanings in Japanese. For example, in Tokyo Japanese, あめ **ame** means *rain* if the first syllable is in high pitch and the second syllable is in low pitch, but it means *candy* if the first syllable is in low pitch and the second syllable is in high pitch. Such a difference cannot be represented by the kana system, but the context can clarify the meanings. Furthermore, words written in kanji are distinct. For example, the word *rain* is 雨 (あめ **ame**), and the word *candy* is 飴 (あめ **ame**).

EXERCISE
1·1

*Read the hiragana and katakana characters in the table on page 1, from left to right, row by row, from the top row to the bottom row, paying attention to the pronunciation, as in **a, i, u, e, o, ka, ki, ku** . . .*

The first 10 hiragana

The first 10 hiragana include five syllables that are just vowels, **a, i, u, e,** and **o,** and five syllables with the consonant **k,** which are **ka, ki, ku, ke,** and **ko.**

*Practice writing the first 10 hiragana characters, paying attention to the order and direction of the strokes. Be careful because the hiragana characters あ **a** and お **o** are similar in shape. In some fonts, the third and the fourth strokes in the hiragana き **ki** are connected, appearing as き, but they are usually separate when this character is handwritten.*

あ　あ　————　————　————
い　い　————　————　————
う　う　————　————　————
え　え　————　————　————
お　お　————　————　————
か　か　————　————　————
き　き　————　————　————
く　く　————　————　————
け　け　————　————　————
こ　こ　————　————　————

Read the following sequences of hiragana, row by row. Do not move on to a new row until you are able to read the current row very quickly. Repeat as many times as you need until you can read them very smoothly. You may try to read them backward for additional practice.

あいあいう

あいうえあうい

おあうあお

かきかきく

くきけくきくこ

こけこきか

あかあおあ

いきけきえけき

おこえこけ

The following are some words that can be written using some of the first 10 hiragana characters. Read them aloud. For a greater challenge, cover the romaji as you work on this exercise. You may find it strange to have multiple syllables that are just vowels within a word, so watch out!

1.	*love*	あい	**ai**
2.	*red*	あか	**aka**
3.	*house*	いえ	**ie**
4.	*squid*	いか	**ika**
5.	*train station*	えき	**eki**
6.	*top*	うえ	**ue**
7.	*face*	かお	**kao**
8.	*oyster*	かき	**kaki**
9.	*chrysanthemum*	きく	**kiku**
10.	*carp*	こい	**koi**

Write the hiragana for the following words. Refer to the romaji in the table on page 1.

1.	*shellfish*	**kai**	_____
2.	*pond*	**ike**	_____
3.	*hill*	**oka**	_____
4.	*autumn*	**aki**	_____
5.	*blue*	**ao**	_____

The second 10 hiragana

The second 10 hiragana characters include five syllables with the consonant **s** and five syllables with the consonant **t**. When the vowel is **i**, we get **shi** and **chi** rather than **si** and **ti**. When the vowel is **u**, we get **tsu** rather than **tu**.

EXERCISE 1·6

Practice writing the second 10 hiragana characters, paying attention to the order and direction of the strokes. Note that the second and the third strokes of the hiragana さ ***sa*** *are connected in some fonts, as in* さ*, appearing like a mirror-image of the hiragana* ち ***chi****, but they are usually separate when this character is handwritten.*

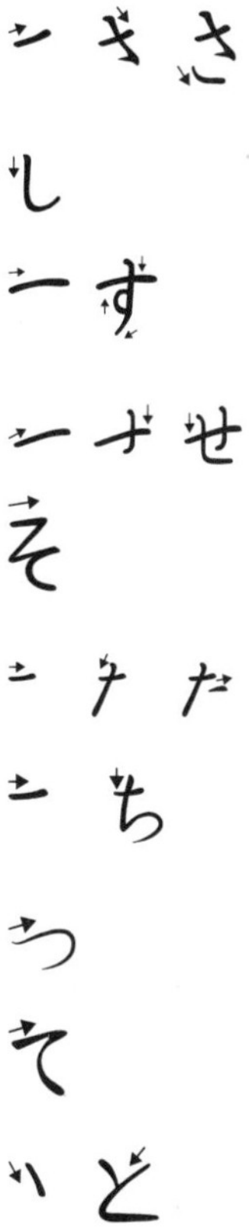

さ さ ______ ______ ______ ______

し し ______ ______ ______ ______

す す ______ ______ ______ ______

せ せ ______ ______ ______ ______

そ そ ______ ______ ______ ______

た た ______ ______ ______ ______

ち ち ______ ______ ______ ______

つ つ ______ ______ ______ ______

て て ______ ______ ______ ______

と と ______ ______ ______ ______

EXERCISE 1·7

Read the following sequences of hiragana, row by row. Do not move on to a new row until you are able to read the current row very quickly. Repeat as many times as you need until you can read them very smoothly. You may try to read them backward for additional practice.

さしさしす

すせそすせそす

しさそすせ

たちちたつ

つちてとちてと

たてとつち

さちさちき

えせてせえせて

おこそとこ

いきしちき

あかさたかさた

うくすつす

The following are some words that can be written using some of the first 20 hiragana characters. Read them aloud. For a greater challenge, cover the romaji as you work on this exercise.

1. *cow*	うし	**ushi**
2. *lie*	うそ	**uso**
3. *umbrella*	かさ	**kasa**
4. *sushi*	すし	**sushi**
5. *world*	せかい	**sekai**
6. *octopus*	たこ	**tako**
7. *subway*	ちかてつ	**chikatetsu**
8. *moon*	つき	**tsuki**

Write the hiragana for the following words. Refer to the romaji in the table on page 1.

1. *soil*	**tsuchi**	_____
2. *home*	**uchi**	_____
3. *hand*	**te**	_____
4. *eagle*	**taka**	_____
5. *basement*	**chika**	_____
6. *iron*	**tetsu**	_____

The third 10 hiragana

The third 10 hiragana include five syllables with the consonant **n** and five syllables with the consonant **h**. However, remember that ふ is not pronounced as **hu** but as **fu**.

Practice writing the third 10 hiragana characters, paying attention to the order and direction of the strokes.

ニ ナ ナ゙ な　な　な ——— ——— ——— ——— ———
い ゛ に　に　に ——— ——— ——— ——— ———
へ ぬ　ぬ　ぬ ——— ——— ——— ——— ———
ヿ ね　ね　ね ——— ——— ——— ——— ———
の　の　の ——— ——— ——— ——— ———
し゛ に゛ば　は　は ——— ——— ——— ——— ———
ひ　ひ　ひ ——— ——— ——— ——— ———
゛ ゛゛ ぶ　ふ　ふ ——— ——— ——— ——— ———
へ　へ　へ ——— ——— ——— ——— ———
し゛ に゛ ぼ　ほ　ほ ——— ——— ——— ——— ———

Read the following sequences of hiragana, row by row. Do not move on to a new row until you are able to read the current row very quickly. Repeat as many times as you need until you can read them very smoothly. You may try to read them backward for additional practice.

なになにぬ

ぬねぬねなにの

のにねぬな

はひはひふ

ふへひへふへほ

ほはひへふ

あかさたな

なたさかはなた

いきしちに

せてねへけえね

ほことこい

ははほはほぬ

くへしつてのつ

はなさかな

EXERCISE
1·12

Read the following words, which are written using some of the first 30 hiragana characters. For a greater challenge, cover the romaji as you work on this exercise.

1.	dog	いぬ	**inu**
2.	fish	さかな	**sakana**
3.	sand	すな	**suna**
4.	summer	なつ	**natsu**
5.	meat	にく	**niku**
6.	cat	ねこ	**neko**
7.	flower	はな	**hana**
8.	fire	ひ	**hi**
9.	ship	ふね	**fune**
10.	star	ほし	**hoshi**

EXERCISE
1·13

Write the hiragana for the following words. Refer to the romaji in the table on page 1.

1.	chopsticks	**hashi**	_____
2.	country	**kuni**	_____
3.	pear	**nashi**	_____
4.	hole	**ana**	_____
5.	grave	**haka**	_____

The last 16 hiragana

The remaining 16 characters in the table on page 1 include five syllables with the consonant **m**, three syllables with the consonant **y**, five syllables with the consonant **r**, and **wa** and **n**. In Japanese, the **y** sound does not contrast meaning when placed before the vowels **i** or **e**. That's why **yi** and **ye** are missing from the hiragana table. Similarly, the consonant **w** can contrast meaning only if it appears before the vowel **a** in the hiragana system. That's why **wi**, **wu**, and **we** are missing from the hiragana table. **Wo** (を) does appear in the table, but it is used only for the direct object particle, and it actually sounds like **o**. As discussed earlier, the Japanese **r** is very different from the English *r*. It is closer to the English *l* but not quite the same. The consonant **n** can form an independent syllable (or **mora**, in linguistic terms). Note that the two strokes of the hiragana り **ri** are connected in some fonts, as in り, but they are usually separate when this character is handwritten.

EXERCISE
1·14

Practice writing the last 16 hiragana characters, paying attention to the order and direction of the strokes.

ー ニ ま　ま　ま　_____ _____ _____

み　み　み　_____ _____ _____

む　む　む　_____ _____ _____

め　め　め　_____ _____ _____

も　も　も　_____ _____ _____

や　や　や　_____ _____ _____

ゆ　ゆ　ゆ　_____ _____ _____

よ　よ　よ　_____ _____ _____

ら　ら　ら　_____ _____ _____

り　り　り　_____ _____ _____

る　る　る　_____ _____ _____

れ　れ　れ　_____ _____ _____

ろ　ろ　ろ　_____ _____ _____

わ　わ　わ　_____ _____ _____

こそを　をを　—　—　—　—　—　—
ん　　　んん　—　—　—　—　—

Read the following sequences of hiragana, row by row. Do not move on to a new row until you are able to read the current row very quickly. Repeat as many times as you need until you can read them very smoothly. You may try to read them backward for additional practice.

まみまみむ

むめもまもめむ

もまもまむ

やゆよやよ

らりらりるりら

れろるろる

われんわね

はまやらわらや

ふむゆるぬ

すぬなはほ

らろるろられを

ぬめあおぬ

Basic vocabulary with simple sounds

Now that you are familiar with all of the basic kana characters, you can combine them into some basic Japanese words.

Words for body parts

Many of the vocabulary words for body parts are easy to pronounce. Practice saying each one as you point to the appropriate part of the body.

foot/leg	あし	**ashi**
head	あたま	**atama**
belly	おなか	**onaka**
face	かお	**kao**
mouth	くち	**kuchi**
back	せなか	**senaka**
nose	はな	**hana**
ear	みみ	**mimi**
eye	め	**me**

Words for nature

As you practice saying these Japanese words for nature, picture them. For example, as you say あめ, picture rain falling.

あめ	**ame**	*rain*
いし	**ishi**	*stone*
いわ	**iwa**	*rock*
うみ	**umi**	*ocean*
かわ	**kawa**	*river*
き	**ki**	*tree*
くも	**kumo**	*cloud*
そら	**sora**	*sky*
たに	**tani**	*valley*
つき	**tsuki**	*the moon*
つち	**tsuchi**	*soil*
ひ	**hi**	*fire*
ほし	**hoshi**	*star*
やま	**yama**	*mountain*
ゆき	**yuki**	*snow*

EXERCISE

1·16

Choose the correct English translation from the options in parentheses.

1. め   (eye, mouth, nose, ear)

2. みみ   (eye, mouth, nose, ear)

3. くち   (eye, mouth, nose, ear)

4. はな   (eye, mouth, nose, ear)

5. あし   (head, belly, foot, back)

6. あたま   (face, head, hand, foot)

EXERCISE

1·17

Match the Japanese words and their English counterparts.

1. やま _____   a. *ocean*

2. そら _____   b. *sky*

3. かわ _____   c. *mountain*

4. うみ _____   d. *river*

Write the following words in Japanese.

1. *mouth* _____

2. *head* _____

3. *mountain* _____

4. *river* _____

5. *star* _____

Double consonants, long vowels, and family terms

Here you will learn how to represent double consonants and long vowels, and then you will see them used in words that Japanese use to address older family members.

Small つ

To represent the brief abrupt pause found in double consonants, use the small つ. For example, **kitte** (*postage stamp)* is written as きって.

Adding a vowel

Together, a hiragana character and the vowel **o** followed by う **u** jointly form a syllable that sounds like the long vowel **ō**. So, おとうさん (*father*) is read as **otōsan**. Similarly, a hiragana character with a vowel **e** followed by い **i** jointly form a syllable that sounds like the long vowel **ē**. For example, せんせい (*teacher*) is read as **sensē**. (However, in this book, **ē** in such cases is still specified as **ei** in romaji, as in **sensei**, following the common practice in most romaji Japanese dictionaries.)

Addressing older family members

The Japanese address their older family members by using the following kinship terms, although they address their younger family members by using their given name or nickname.

father	おとうさん	**otōsan**
mother	おかあさん	**okāsan**
older brother	おにいさん	**onīsan**
older sister	おねえさん	**onēsan**

Read the following words written in hiragana aloud. For a greater challenge, cover the romaji as you work on this exercise.

1.	*teacher*	せんせい	**sensei**
2.	*ice*	とおり	**kōri**
3.	*street*	とうり	**tōri**
4.	*postage stamp*	きって	**kitte**

Write the following words in hiragana.

1. *father* _____

2. *mother* _____

3. *older brother* _____

4. *older sister* _____

Diacritics for voiced and plosive sounds and food terms

Two diacritics, ゛ and ゜, are used to represent additional syllable sounds that can contribute to the meaning of Japanese words. Here you will learn how to use these diacritics and then see them used in some Japanese food terms.

Diacritics ゛ and ゜

By adding the diacritic mark ゛ at the upper-right corner of a certain character, you can indicate that its beginning consonant is voiced. By adding the mark ゜ at the upper-right corner of a certain character, you change its beginning consonant to **p**. Note that ゛ changes **h** and **f** to **b**. The syllable **ji** is usually represented by じ, and it is also represented by ぢ in limited cases. Similarly, the syllable **zu** is usually represented by ず, and it is also represented by づ in limited cases. The following table shows which characters they are combined with and how they are read:

が ga	ぎ gi	ぐ gu	げ ge	ご go
ざ za	じ ji	ず zu	ぜ ze	ぞ zo
だ da	ぢ ji	づ zu	で de	ど do
ば ba	び bi	ぶ bu	べ be	ぼ bo
ぱ pa	ぴ pi	ぷ pu	ぺ pe	ぽ po

Names of Japanese food

Japanese food is popular overseas. You might see some of the following on the menu at a Japanese restaurant in your country:

sushi	すし	**sushi**
sashimi (sliced raw fish)	さしみ	**sashimi**
tempura (deep-fried battered seafood, vegetables, and mushrooms)	てんぷら	**tenpura**
sukiyaki (beef stew in the Japanese style)	すきやき	**sukiyaki**
buckwheat noodle	そば	**soba**
thick white noodle	うどん	**udon**

EXERCISE 1·21

Practice writing the following Japanese words.

すし   _____ _____ _____ _____

さしみ _____ _____ _____ _____

てんぷら _____ _____ _____ _____

すきやき _____ _____ _____ _____

そば   _____ _____ _____ _____

うどん _____ _____ _____ _____

Palatalized sounds

Palatalized sounds are pronounced with the body of the tongue raised toward the palate. Here you will learn how to represent these sounds and see their use in familiar Japanese words.

Using small や **ya**, ゆ **yu**, or よ **yo**

To express a palatalized sound like **kya** or **hyu**, use a character that represents the initial consonant and the vowel **i** and then add small-sized や **ya**, ゆ **yu**, or よ **yo**, depending on the vowel needed. The following table shows how to represent palatalized syllables in both hiragana and katakana:

きゃ kya	きゅ kyu	きょ kyo
ぎゃ gya	ぎゅ gyu	ぎょ gyo
しゃ sha	しゅ shu	しょ sho
じゃ ja	じゅ ju	じょ jo
ちゃ cha	ちゅ chu	ちょ cho
ぢゃ ja	ぢゅ ju	ぢょ jo
にゃ nya	にゅ nyu	にょ nyo
ひゃ hya	ひゅ hyu	ひょ hyo
びゃ bya	びゅ byu	びょ byo
ぴゃ pya	ぴゅ pyu	ぴょ pyo
みゃ mya	みゅ myu	みょ myo
りゃ rya	りゅ ryu	りょ ryo

Japanese words you might already know

The following words related to Japanese culture might be already familiar to you:

calligraphy	しょどう	**shodō**
flower arranging	いけばな	**ikebana**
judo	じゅうどう	**jūdō**
karate	からて	**karate**
kendo (Japanese fencing)	けんどう	**kendō**
kimono	きもの	**kimono**
manga	マンガ	**comic books**
origami	おりがみ	**origami**
tea ceremony (chado)	さどう	**sadō**

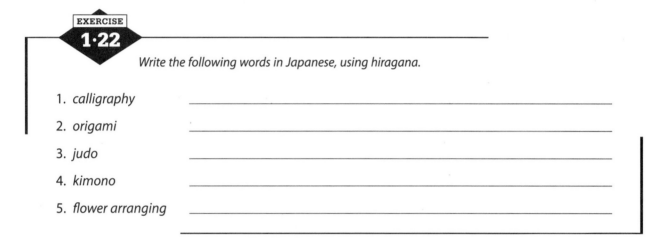

EXERCISE
1·22

Write the following words in Japanese, using hiragana.

1. *calligraphy* _____

2. *origami* _____

3. *judo* _____

4. *kimono* _____

5. *flower arranging* _____

EXERCISE
1·23

Read the following place names written in hiragana and guess what they are.

1. とうきょう _____

2. きょうと _____

3. おおさか _____

Reading basic katakana

Each hiragana character was created by simplifying or deforming some kanji character, and each katakana character was created by taking a part of some kanji. Whereas hiragana characters have more curved lines, katakana characters have more straight lines and angles. The following table shows pairs of hiragana and katakana and the stroke order of katakana characters:

あ	ア	⌐ア	つ	ツ	ヽ ヾ ツ	も	モ	ニ モ
い	イ	ノ イ	て	テ	一 二 テ	や	ヤ	フ ヤ
う	ウ	ヽ ゛ ウ	と	ト	｜ ト	ゆ	ユ	ユ ユ
え	エ	一 下 エ	な	ナ	一 ナ	よ	ヨ	ヨ ヨ ヨ
お	オ	一 ナ オ	に	ニ	一 二	よ	ヨ	ユ ユ
か	カ	フ カ	ぬ	ヌ	フ ヌ	よ	ヨ	ヨ ヨ ヨ
き	キ	一 二 キ	ね	ネ	｀ ウ ネ ネ	ら	ラ	一 ラ
く	ク	ノ ク	の	ノ	ノ	り	リ	｜ リ
け	ケ	ノ ケ ケ	は	ハ	ノ ハ	る	ル	｜ ル
こ	コ	フ コ	ひ	ヒ	一 ヒ	れ	レ	レ
さ	サ	一 十 サ	ふ	フ	フ	ろ	ロ	｜ フ ロ
し	シ	ヽ ヽ シ	へ	ヘ	ヘ	わ	ワ	｜ ワ
す	ス	フ ス	ほ	ホ	一 ナ オ ホ	を	ヲ	一 二 ヲ
せ	セ	ヒ セ	ま	マ	フ マ	ん	ン	ヽ ン
そ	ソ	ヽ ソ	み	ミ	ヽ ヽ ミ			
た	タ	ノ ク タ	む	ム	ム ム			
ち	チ	ノ 二 チ	め	メ	ノ メ			

Look at the preceding table and list the katakana characters that conform to the following descriptions.

1. Katakana characters that have only one stroke: _____

2. Katakana characters that have two separate simple horizontal lines: _____

3. Katakana characters that look similar to the hiragana counterparts: _____

Read the following pairs of katakana characters and write out in Japanese. They look similar, so be careful.

1. シ and ツ　_____

2. ン and ソ　_____

3. ク and ケ　_____

4. ク and ワ　_____

5. ク and タ　_____

6. ロ and コ　_____

7. ル and レ　_____

8. チ and テ　_____

Read the following words written in katakana and guess what they mean. Refer to the table on page 16, as needed.

1. テスト　_____

2. カメラ　_____

3. ネクタイ　_____

4. ホテル　_____

Read the following words written in katakana aloud, paying attention to the diacritics.

1.	*TV*	テレビ	**terebi**
2.	*radio*	ラジオ	**rajio**
3.	*computer, PC*	パソコン	**pasokon**
4.	*convenience store*	コンビニ	**konbini**
5.	*pen*	ペン	**pen**

Read the following words written in katakana aloud, paying attention to long vowels and double consonants. Remember that the elongation mark (一) represents a long vowel.

1. *boat*	ボート	**bōto**
2. *pet*	ペット	**petto**
3. *internet*	インターネット	**intānetto**
4. *soccer*	サッカー	**sakkā**

Special katakana combinations

The katakana system allows some combinations of characters that are not available in the hiragana system because katakana is used to represent non-Japanese names and words. Examples include:

che	チェ	(チェス *chess*)
di	ディ	(アンディー *Andy*)
du	デュ	(デュエット *duet*)
fa	ファ	(ソファー *sofa*)
fe	フェ	(カフェ *cafe*)
fi	フィ	(フィアンセ *fiancé*)
fo	フォ	(フォーク *fork*)
je	ジェ	(ジェットコースター *rollercoaster*)
she	シェ	(シェークスピア *Shakespeare*)
ti	ティ	(ティーシャツ *T-shirt*)
tsa	ツァ	(モッツァレッラ *mozzarella*)
tu	トゥ	(トゥール *Tours*)
va	ヴァ	(ヴァイオリン *violin*)
ve	ヴェ	(ヴェルヴェット *velvet*)
vo	ヴォ	(ヴォーカル *vocal*)
we	ウェ	(ウェーター *waiter*)
wi	ウィ	(ウィーン *Vienna*)
wo	ウォ	(ウォークマン *Walkman*)

Country names written in katakana

Country names are written in katakana. The exceptions are country names that are conventionally written in kanji. You or some of your friends may be from these countries.

Australia	オーストラリア	**Ōsutoraria**
Canada	カナダ	**Kanada**
France	フランス	**Furansu**
India	インド	**Indo**
Russia	ロシア	**Roshia**
United States of America	アメリカ	**Amerika**

EXERCISE 1·29

Read the following city names written in katakana. For a greater challenge, cover the romaji as you work on this exercise.

1. *Toronto*	トロント	**Toronto**
2. *Boston*	ボストン	**Bosuton**
3. *London*	ロンドン	**Rondon**
4. *Vancouver*	バンクーバー	**Bankūbā**
5. *Melbourne*	メルボルン	**Meruborun**

EXERCISE 1·30

Read the following words that name Western food and beverages. For a greater challenge, cover the romaji as you work on this exercise.

1. *hamburger*	ハンバーガー	**hanbāgā**
2. *hotdog*	ホットドッグ	**hottodoggu**
3. *pancake*	パンケーキ	**pankēki**
4. *coffee*	コーヒー	**kōhī**
5. *orange juice*	オレンジジュース	**orenjijūsu**
6. *fondue*	フォンデュ	**fondu**

EXERCISE 1·31

Write the following country names in katakana.

1. *United States of America* _____

2. *Canada* _____

3. *Russia* _____

4. *France* _____

Writing sentences

Here are some rules for writing Japanese sentences:

1. The Japanese text can be written from left to right and top to bottom, as in English, but it can also be written from top to bottom and right to left. The Japanese period is 。, and the Japanese comma is 、 or , .

2. The character を is used only as a particle marking a direct object in modern Japanese. The character を is pronounced as **o**, just like お. Some people pronounce を as **wo** when reading a kana chart, but they still pronounce it as **o** in sentences.

3. When the character は is used as a topic marker, its pronunciation is **wa** rather than **ha**. When the character へ is used as a direction-marking particle, it is read as **e** rather than as **he**.

Read the following sentences out loud. For a greater challenge, cover the romaji as you work on this exercise.

1. エミリーはすしをたべました。

   Emirī wa sushi o tabemashita.

   Emily ate sushi.

2. ボストンへいきますが、とまりません。

   Bosuton e ikimasu ga, tomarimasen.

   I'll go to Boston but won't stay there overnight.

Kanji

Most kanji characters can be pronounced in both Japanese and Chinese ways. For example, the Japanese way of pronouncing 人 is **hito**, and the Chinese way of pronouncing it is **nin** or **jin**. There is no standard rule for the difference, so you need to learn each one individually. In this book, romaji shows how kanji characters are read in each phrase and sentence.

The following table shows some simple kanji characters that are frequently used as components of other kanji characters:

English Word	Kanji	Stroke Order	Usage Examples
person	人	ノ 人	人 **hito** (*person*); 日本人 **Ni-hon-jin** (*a Japanese person*); アメリカ人 **Amerika-jin** (*an American person*); 三人 **san-nin** (*three people*)
mountain	山	丨 山 山	山 **yama** (*mountain*); 山田 **Yama-da** (*Yamada, a family name*); 富士山 **Fu-ji-san** (*Mt. Fuji*)

English Word	Kanji	Stroke Order	Usage Examples
river	川	丿 丿丨 川	川 **kawa** (*river*); 川口 **Kawa-guchi** (*Kawaguchi*, a family name)
sun	日	刂 冂 冃 日	日 **hi** (*the sun*); 日本 **Ni-hon** or **Nip-pon** (*Japan*); 日曜日 **Nichi-yō-bi** (*Sunday*)
mouth	口	丨 冖 口	口 **kuchi** (*mouth*); 人口 **jin-kō** (*population*)
tree	木	一 十 才 木	木 **ki** (*tree*); 木曜日 **Moku-yō-bi** (*Thursday*)
fire	火	丶 丷 少 火	火 **hi** (*fire*); 火曜日 **Ka-yō-bi** (*Tuesday*)
soil	土	一 十 土	土 **tsuchi** (*soil*); 土曜日 **Do-yō-bi** (*Saturday*)
water	水	亅 刋 氺 水	水 **mizu** (*water*); 水曜日 **Sui-yō-bi** (*Wednesday*)
moon	月	丿 冂 月 月	月 **tsuki** (*the moon*); 月曜日 **Getsu-yō-bi** (*Monday*)

Kanji characters that represent verbs and adjectives need to be followed by hiragana that show inflectional endings, as in 書く **kaku** (*write*) and 書いた **kaita** (*wrote*). The following are some frequently used verbs written in kanji and hiragana. A dash in romaji separates the portion that represents kanji and the portion that represents hiragana.

go	行く	**i-ku**
come	来る	**ku-ru**
return	帰る	**kae-ru**
change	変える	**ka-eru**
read	読む	**yo-mu**
write	書く	**ka-ku**
walk	歩く	**aru-ku**
buy	買う	**ka-u**

The following are some frequently used adjectives written in kanji and hiragana:

expensive	高い	**taka-i**
cheap	安い	**yasu-i**
quiet	静かな	**shizu-kana**
fun	楽しい	**tano-shii**
easy	簡単な	**kantan-na**
difficult	難しい	**muzuka-shii**

Practice writing the following basic kanji characters, using the correct stroke order.

person	人	ﾉ	人			
mountain	山	丨	山	山			
river	川	ﾉ	丿ﾞ	川			
sun	日	丨	冂	日	日		
mouth	口	丨	冂	口			
tree	木	一	十	才	木		
fire	火	ヽ	⺌	少	火		
soil	土	一	十	土			
water	水	亅	刁	水	水		
moon	月	ﾉ	冂	月	月		

The following words are written in kanji followed by hiragana in parentheses. Write the English equivalent for each one.

1. 口 (くち) _____

2. 山 (やま) _____

3. 川 (かわ) _____

4. 火 (ひ) _____

5. 月 (つき) _____

6. 木 (き) _____

Getting to know someone ◆·2·

This chapter introduces basic vocabulary words and sentence structures that are needed for identifying people and things.

Introducing yourself with はじめまして Hajimemashite

When you want to introduce yourself to someone, approach him/her and say はじめまして **Hajimemashite**. This literally means *Beginning*, but its function is to clarify the fact that you are meeting the person for the very first time and are willing to get to know him/her. Then say your name and add です **desu** and say 宜しくお願いします **Yoroshiku onegai shimasu**, which literally means *Please be nice to me* but actually shows your modest attitude and your desire to have a good relationship with the person. If someone says this to you, you should respond with こちらこそ宜しくお願いします **Kochira koso yoroshiku onegai shimasu**, which means *It's me who should say that*.

Occupational and respectful titles

When addressing a non-family person, try to use his or her occupational title, such as 先生 **sensei** (teacher) or 社長 **shachō** (company president), after his or her family name. If an occupational title is not available, use a respectful title such as さん **san** after his or her family name or given name. There are additional respectful titles, but さん **san** is most neutral and versatile. Make sure not to use an occupational title or a respectful title after your name, even if other people keep addressing you with them. The following are some examples of occupational titles and their use with the family name **Tanaka**:

Professors, teachers, medical doctors, lawyers, etc.	先生	**sensei**	田中先生	**Tanaka sensei**
Company president	社長	**shachō**	田中社長	**Tanaka shachō**
Division manager	部長	**buchō**	田中部長	**Tanaka buchō**

The following are some respectful titles:

neutral (for most adults)	. . . さん	. . . **san**
affectionate (for children)	. . . ちゃん	. . . **chan**
business-like (for clients)	. . . 様	. . . **sama**

EXERCISE
2·1

Jane White introduces herself to Keiko Hayashi at a party. Complete their conversation.

WHITE　はじめまして。ホワイトです。宜しくお願いします。

Hajimemashite. Howaito desu. Yoroshiku onegai shimasu.

HAYASHI　ホワイトさんですか。

Howaito-san desu ka.

WHITE　はい。

Hai.

HAYASHI　はじめまして。林です。＿＿＿＿＿＿＿＿＿ 宜しくお願いします。

Hajimemashite. Hayashi desu. ＿＿＿＿＿＿＿＿＿ yoroshiku onegai shimasu.

Asking どちらからですか Dochira kara desu ka (*Where are you from?*)

After you introduce yourself to someone for the first time, you might next want to ask the person where he/she is from. Here you'll learn how to do that.

The question word どちら dochira and the particle から kara

どちら **dochira** literally means *which way* but is also used as a polite version of どこ **doko** (*where*). から **kara** is the particle that means *from*. If you are from Boston, you can say ボストンからです **Bosuton kara desu** (*I'm from Boston.*). To find out where a person is from, you can ask どちらからですか **Dochira kara desu ka** (*Where are you from?*).

Personal pronouns あなた anata, 私 watashi, and 僕 boku

When you are asking someone where he/she is from, you do not need to say あなた **anata** (*you*) because it would be obvious, unnatural, and sound like translation. Instead, you can say the name of the person you are talking to. For example, if you are talking to Ms. Hayashi, you can ask her **Hayashi-san wa dochira kara desu ka**, which means *Where are you from, Ms. Hayashi?* It is fine to use 私 **watashi** to refer to yourself. If you are a male, you may also use 僕 **boku** to refer to yourself.

Names for countries, regions, and cities

If someone asks you where you are from, you can answer the question with the name of a country, a region, or a city, depending on the context. The following are names of some countries, regions, and cities:

Australia	オーストラリア	**Ōsutoraria**
Beijing	北京	**Pekin**
California	カリフォルニア	**Kariforunia**
Canada	カナダ	**Kanada**
Chile	チリ	**Chiri**
China	中国	**Chūgoku**

England	イギリス	Igirisu
France	フランス	Furansu
Germany	ドイツ	Doitsu
Hong Kong	香港	Honkon
India	インド	Indo
Italy	イタリア	Itaria
Japan	日本	Nihon, Nippon
Kenya	ケニア	Kenia
Osaka	大阪	Ōsaka
Philippines	フィリピン	Firipin
Russia	ロシア	Roshia
Shanghai	上海	Shanhai
South Korea	韓国	Kankoku
Spain	スペイン	Supein
Taiwan	台湾	Taiwan
Thailand	タイ	Tai
United States of America	アメリカ	Amerika

EXERCISE
2·2

Ms. White asks Ms. Hayashi where she is from. Complete their conversation.

WHITE   林さんは _____ からですか。

Hayashi-san wa _____ kara desu ka.

HAYASHI   私は東京からです。

Watashi wa Tōkyō kara desu.

EXERCISE
2·3

Match the country names written in Japanese with their English equivalents.

1. 日本 **Nihon/Nippon** _____   a. *Canada*

2. アメリカ **Amerika** _____   b. *China*

3. 韓国 **Kankoku** _____   c. *South Korea*

4. 中国 **Chūgoku** _____   d. *United States of America*

5. カナダ **Kanada** _____   e. *Japan*

EXERCISE

2·4

Find nine country names in the puzzle, either vertically (top to bottom) or horizontally (left to right).

ウ	ワ	エ	ク	コ	セ
ル	ロ	サ	ス	フ	イ
カ	シ	イ	ペ	ク	タ
オ	ア	タ	イ	チ	リ
ナ	フ	ラ	ン	ス	ア
ケ	ニ	ア	ド	イ	ツ

EXERCISE

2·5

Translate the following sentences into Japanese.

1. *Meilin (メイリン **Meirin**) is from Beijing.*

_____

2. *Yumiko (由美子 **Yumiko**) is from Tokyo.*

_____

3. *Thomas (トーマス **Tōmasu**) is from Canada (カナダ **Kanada**).*

_____

4. *Emily (エミリー **Emirī**) is from England (イギリス **Igirisu**).*

_____

EXERCISE

2·6

State where you are from in Japanese.

_____

_____

Describing the nationality of a person

Sometimes you want to be able to describe the nationality or language of another person. Here you will learn the proper form as well as the words for some nationalities and languages.

To say "x is y" with . . . は **wa** . . . です **desu**

When describing someone, the first step is to refer to that person and add the topic marker は **wa**, as you have already done in this chapter. For example, if you are talking about Ken, you say ケンさんは **Ken-san wa**. Then you say Ken's nationality—for example, アメリカ人 **Amerika-jin** (*American*)—and add the copular verb です **desu**. For example:

> ケンさんはアメリカ人です。
> **Ken-san wa Amerika-jin desu.**
> *Ken is an American.*

If you want say that someone is not a particular nationality, replace です **desu** with じゃありません **ja arimasen** or with じゃないです **ja nai desu**. For example:

> ケンさんはアメリカ人じゃありません。
> **Ken-san wa Amerika-jin ja arimasen.**

> ケンさんはアメリカ人じゃないです。
> **Ken-san wa Amerika-jin ja nai desu.**
> *Ken is not an American.*

In a formal context or in writing, replace じゃ **ja** in these negative copular verbs with では **de wa**.

To express additional items with . . . も **mo**

If the same situation applies to another person, just use も **mo** to mark the additional person instead of using は **wa**. For example, ビルさんもアメリカ人です **Biru-san mo Amerika-jin desu** means *Bill is also an American*.

Nationality

To refer to a person's nationality, use the country name and add 人 **jin** (*person*). The following are some examples:

American (person)	アメリカ人	**Amerika-jin**
Chinese (person)	中国人	**Chūgoku-jin**
French (person)	フランス人	**Furansu-jin**
Japanese (person)	日本人	**Nihon-jin**
Korean (person)	韓国人	**Kankoku-jin**
Russian (person)	ロシア人	**Roshia-jin**

Languages

To refer to a language, you add 語 **go** (*language*) after the country name (or region name):

Arabic	アラビア語	**Arabia-go**
Cantonese	広東語	**Kanton-go**
Chinese	中国語	**Chūgoku-go**
English	英語	**Ei-go**
French	フランス語	**Furansu-go**
German	ドイツ語	**Doitsu-go**
Hindi	ヒンディー語	**Hindī-go**
Italian	イタリア語	**Itaria-go**
Korean	韓国語	**Kankoku-go**
Mandarin Chinese	北京語	**Pekin-go**
Russian	ロシア語	**Roshia-go**
Spanish	スペイン語	**Supein-go**

EXERCISE
2·7

How do you say the following in Japanese?

1. *an Italian (person)* _____

2. *a Canadian (person)* _____

3. *a Filipino (person)* _____

4. *an Indian (person)* _____

EXERCISE
2·8

Translate the following sentences into Japanese.

1. *Takeshi (武さん **Takeshi-san**) is Japanese.*

_____

2. *Heejeong (ヒージョンさん **Hījon-san**) is Korean.*

_____

3. *Professor Brown (ブラウン先生 **Buraun sensei**) is a Canadian.*

_____

4. *Mr. Chen (チェンさん **Chen-san**) is Chinese.*

_____

5. *Meilin (メイリンさん **Meirin-san**) is also Chinese.*

_____

6. *George (ジョージさん **Jōji-san**) is not an American.*

_____

EXERCISE
2·9

Describe yourself by stating where you are from and your nationality in Japanese.

_____

_____

_____

Referring to someone with あの ano . . .

To refer to a person, the easiest way is to use the person's name. However, if you don't know the name of the person, but your conversational partner can actually see the person, you can use a demonstrative adjective and a common noun. For example, あの人 **ano hito** means *that person over there*.

あの ano

To refer to a person you and your conversational partner can see, use a demonstrative adjective like あの **ano** (*that*) and a common noun like 人 **hito** (*person*) and 学生 **gakusei** (*student*). For example:

> あの人はアメリカ人です
> **Ano hito wa Amerika-jin desu.**
> *That person (over there) is an American.*

Additional demonstrative adjectives are discussed later in this chapter.

Words for people

It is useful to know a common noun like 人 **hito** so you can refer to someone as *that person, that man,* or *that girl.* The following are some common nouns for people:

boy	男の子	**otoko no ko**
child	子ども	**kodomo**
girl	女の子	**onna no ko**
man	男の人	**otoko no hito**
person	人	**hito**
woman	女の人	**onna no hito**

EXERCISE
2·10

Translate the following sentences into Japanese.

1. *That woman is Japanese.*

   _____

2. *That man is Chinese.*

   _____

3. *That person is Korean.*

   _____

4. *That child is French.*

   _____

Describing the occupation of a person

When you meet a person for the first time, you may want to talk about your job or where you work.

Creating a modifier using a noun and の **no**

To tell someone you are a student, you can say 学生 **gakusei** (*student*). But if you want to add what kind of student, add a word before it and mark it with the particle の **no**. For example, 日本語の 学生 **nihongo no gakusei** means a *student of Japanese*.

Words for occupation

The following are some nouns for occupation:

doctor	医者	**isha**
lawyer	弁護士	**bengoshi**
nurse	看護師	**kangoshi**
store worker	店員	**ten'in**
student	学生	**gakusei**
teacher	先生 / 教師	**sensei/kyōshi**

When you are describing yourself or your family, use 教師 **kyōshi** instead of 先生 **sensei**.

EXERCISE
2·11

Translate the following sentences into Japanese.

1. *Mr. Mori* (森さん **Mori-san**) *is a lawyer.*

   _____

2. *That person is a Japanese student (a student who is studying the Japanese language).*

   _____

3. *That person is a Japanese student (a student whose nationality is Japanese).*

   _____

4. *That woman is a teacher.*

   _____

5. *That woman is a Japanese teacher (a teacher of the Japanese language).*

   _____

Words for institutions

When you describe a person's occupation, you can say where the person works. For example, if someone is a high school teacher, you can say either 高校の先生です **Kōkō no sensei desu** (*He is a high school teacher*) or 高校で働いています **Kōkō de hataraite imasu** (*He works at a high school*). The following is a list of types of institutions:

bank	銀行	**ginkō**
city hall	市役所	**shiyakusho**
company	会社	**kaisha**
department store	デパート	**depāto**
elementary school	小学校	**shōgakkō**
factory	工場	**kōjō**

fire station	消防署	**shōbōsho**
graduate school	大学院	**daigakuin**
high school	高校	**kōkō**
hospital	病院	**byōin**
library	図書館	**toshokan**
middle school	中学校	**chūgakkō**
police station	警察署	**keisatsusho**
restaurant	レストラン	**resutoran**
school	学校	**gakkō**
university	大学	**daigaku**

EXERCISE 2·12

Translate the following sentences into English.

1. ブラウンさんは高校の日本語の先生です。

   Buraun-san wa kōkō no Nihongo no sensei desu.

   _____

2. 田中さんは自動車の工場で働いています。

   Tanaka-san wa jidōsha no kōjō de hataraite imasu.

   (自動車 **jidōsha** means *automobile*)

   _____

3. マイクさんはデパートの店員です。

   Maiku-san wa depāto no ten'in desu.

   _____

EXERCISE 2·13

Translate the following sentences into Japanese.

1. *Ms. Ishida* (石田さん **Ishida-san**) *is a college student.*

   _____

2. *Mr. Tani* (谷さん **Tani-san**) *works at a hospital.*

   _____

3. *Ms. Ueda* (上田さん **Ueda-san**) *is an English teacher at a high school in Japan.*

   _____

Talking about family members

To refer to your own family members, use the plain forms. To refer to someone else's family members, use the polite forms. You can also use the polite forms for addressing your own family members who are older than you. (See Chapter 1 for how to address one's older family members.) The following table shows the plain forms and the polite forms you can use for referring to your close family members:

	PLAIN	POLITE
father	父 chichi	お父さん otōsan
mother	母 haha	お母さん okāsan
older brother	兄 ani	お兄さん onīsan
older sister	姉 ane	お姉さん onēsan
younger brother	弟 otōto	弟さん otōtosan
younger sister	妹 imōto	妹さん imōtosan

EXERCISE

2·14

Read the following passage, written by Sachiko, and answer the questions that follow.

私の父は中国人です。 母は日本人です。 父は東京の銀行で働いています。 母は横浜の高校の英語の教師です。 兄はアメリカの大学の経済学の学生です。

Watashi no chichi wa Chūgoku-jin desu. Haha wa Nihon-jin desu. Chichi wa Tōkyō no ginkō de hataraite imasu. Haha wa Yokohama no kōkō no eigo no kyōshi desu. Ani wa Amerika no daigaku no keizaigaku no gakusei desu.

(経済学 **keizaigaku** means *economics*)

1. What is the nationality of Sachiko's father?

   _____

2. What is the nationality of Sachiko's mother?

   _____

3. What does her father do for living?

   _____

4. What does her mother do for living?

   _____

5. What does her brother do now?

   _____

For each of the following, choose the appropriate answer from the options in parentheses.

1. 山田さんの（姉, お姉さん）は看護師です。

   Yamada-san no (ane, onēsan) wa kangoshi desu.

2. 私の（父, お父さん）はアメリカ人です。

   Watashi no (chichi, otōsan) wa Amerika-jin desu.

3. あの人は（日本語, 日本人）です。

   Ano hito wa (Nihon-go, Nihon-jin) desu.

4. 兄は（日本語の学生, 学生の日本語）です。

   Ani wa (Nihon-go no gakusei, gakusei no Nihon-go) desu.

5. 私は（ケン, ケンさん）です。

   Watashi wa (Ken, Ken-san) desu.

Asking questions

When asking a question in Japanese, you do not need to invert the subject and the verb. Here you learn how to ask and answer simple questions.

Asking yes/no questions

To ask a yes/no question, just add the question particle か **ka** at the end of the statement sentence. For example:

> ケンさんはアメリカ人ですか。
> **Ken-san wa Amerika-jin desu ka.**
> *Is Ken an American?*

You don't need a question mark (?) in Japanese, although it is very frequently used.

Answering with "yes" or "no"

The answer to a yes/no question usually starts with はい **hai** or いいえ **ie**. はい **hai** means *correct* or *right*, so if the question is an affirmative question, it means *yes*. いいえ **ie** means *wrong*, so if the question is an affirmative question, it means *no*. Their meanings are reversed in answering negative questions.

The following are possible replies to the affirmative question ケンさんはアメリカ人ですか **Ken-san wa Amerika-jin desu ka** (*Are you an American, Ken?*):

> はい, アメリカ人です。
> **Hai, Amerika-jin desu.**
> *Yes, I'm an American.*

> いいえ, アメリカ人じゃありません。
> **Īe, Amerika-jin ja arimasen.**
> *No, I'm not an American.*

The following are possible replies to the negative question これはいりませんか **Kore wa irimasen ka** (*Don't you need this?*):

> はい, いりません。
> **Hai, irimasen.**
> *Right, I don't need it. (No, I don't need it.)*

> いいえ, いります。
> **Īe, irimasu.**
> *Wrong, I need it. (Yes, I need it.)*

(See Chapter 4 for the verb ending ます **masu** and ません **masen**.)

As you can see, it is very common to omit understood phrases or pronouns in Japanese in replies.

Asking "who?"

To ask "who?" use the question word だれ **dare** or its polite version, どなた **donata**. For example:

> あの人はだれですか。
> **Ano hito wa dare desu ka.**
> *Who is that person?*

The topic particle は **wa** cannot be used for question words, so never say だれは **dare wa** or どなたは **donata wa**.

EXERCISE
2·16

Reorder the items in each set to form a grammatical sentence and then translate it.

1. です **desu**, 私 **watashi**, 学生 **gakusei**, は **wa**

_____

_____

2. 母 **haha**, 看護師 **kangoshi**, は **wa**, です **desu**

_____

_____

3. 中国人 **Chūgoku-jin**, は **wa**, じゃありません **ja arimasen**, チェンさん **Chen-san**

_____

_____

4. 韓国人 **Kankoku-jin**, です **desu**, は **wa**, の **no**, お母さん **okāsan**, チェンさん **Chen-san**

_____

_____

5. 人 **hito**, あの **ano**, です **desu**, は **wa**, か **ka**, だれ **dare**

_____

_____

6. 山田さん **Yamada-san**, 人 **hito**, あの **ano**, 妹さん **imōtosan**, です **desu**, は **wa**, の **no**

_____

_____

_____

EXERCISE
2·17

Read the following passage and state whether each of the sentences that follows is true or false.

チェンさんは私の友達です。　チェンさんは中国人です。　日本語の学生です。　チェンさんのお母さんは看護師です。　チェンさんのお父さんは英語の先生です。　チェンさんのお兄さんは東京の広告の会社の社員です。

Chen-san wa watashi no tomodachi desu. Chen-san wa Chūgoku-jin desu. Nihon-go no gakusei desu. Chen-san no okāsan wa kangoshi desu. Chen-san no otōsan wa eigo no sensei desu. Chen-san no onīsan wa Tōkyō no kōkoku no kaisha no shain desu.

(. . . 広告 **kōkoku** means *advertisement*; の社員 **no shain** means *company employee at . . .*)

1. (True, False): Mr. Chen is a Chinese person.

2. (True, False): Mr. Chen's father works for an automobile company.

3. (True, False): Mr. Chen's mother is a nurse.

4. (True, False): Mr. Chen's older brother is an English teacher.

EXERCISE
2·18

Describe yourself and your family members as much as you can in Japanese.

_____

_____

_____

_____

Two girls, Mika and Alison, are talking. Complete their conversation with the appropriate words.

MIKA   アリソンさんはアメリカ人ですか。

        Arison-san wa Amerika-jin desu ka.

ALISON   _____, 私はアメリカ人です。

        _____, **watashi wa Amerika-jin desu.**

        でも母はアメリカ人じゃ _____。

        Demo haha wa Amerika-jin ja _____.

        フランス人です。

        Furansu-jin desu.

        父はアメリカ人です。

        Chichi wa Amerika-jin desu.

MIKA   ああ, そうですか。

        Ā, sō desu ka.

(でも **demo** means *however;* ああ, そうですか。**Ā, sō desu ka.** means *Oh, I see.*)

Greeting and parting

After you have already met someone for the first time, you use a different greeting than you used upon meeting. You use different forms for greetings depending on the time of day. What you say to a person in parting depends on a number of factors, such as time of day and whether you will see the person again soon.

Greeting

To greet someone in the morning, say おはようございます **Ohayō gozaimasu!** (*Good morning!*). To a close friend or family member, you can just say おはよう **Ohayō!** (*Good morning!*). If it's in the afternoon, say こんにちは **Konnichi wa!**, which means *Good afternoon!* or *Hi!* In the evening, say こんばんは **Konban wa!** (*Good evening!*).

Parting

When you part, you can say じゃあ, また **Jā, mata!** (*See you later!*). If you know that you'll see the person again on the same day or soon, you can say the location and add the particle で **de**, as in じゃあ, またクラスで **Jā, mata kurasu de!** (*I'll see you later in class!*). If it is later in the day and you are unlikely to see the person again on the same day, you may add さようなら **Sayōnara!** (*Bye!*). If you are parting from someone to whom you need to show your respect, you should say しつれいします。 **Shitsurei shimasu.**, which literally translates to *I'll be rude* but actually means that you are leaving. The Japanese do not say さようなら **Sayōnara** to their family. When they leave home in the morning, they say 行ってきます **Itte kimasu!**, which literally means *I'll go and come back.*

Write a Japanese sentence of greeting or parting for each of the following situations.

1. It's 10 AM. You see your teacher at the library.

_____

2. You've just woken up and seen your mother in the kitchen.

_____

3. It's 9 AM and you are about to leave your home for work. Your mother is sending you off.

_____

4. It's 5 PM. You talked with your teacher in her office for 15 minutes. You are ready to leave.

_____

Jane Smith sees Professor Hayashi at the library in the morning. Complete their conversation with the appropriate words.

SMITH   林先生, _____。

    Hayashi sensei, _____.

HAYASHI   ああ, ジェーンさん。おはよう。

    Ā, Jēn-san. Ohayō.

SMITH   じゃあ, またクラスで。_____ します。

    Jā, mata kurasu de. _____ shimasu.

HAYASHI   はい。じゃあ, また。

    Hai. Jā, mata.

Thanking and apologizing

You commonly need to thank people and apologize to them—as well as respond to thanks and apologies. How you do it depends on your relationship.

Saying "thank you"

To thank someone, say ありがとうございます **Arigatō gozaimasu**. To thank deeply, you can add the adverb どうも **dōmo** at the beginning, as in どうもありがとうございます。**Dōmo arigatō gozaimasu**. Never say the short version ありがとう **Arigatō** to anyone except your family, subordinate, or very close friends. On the other hand, you can always say just どうも **Dōmo** to thank anyone without sounding rude. In any case, it is a good idea to slightly bow as you say these phrases.

  Common responses to such phrases of appreciation include いいえ **Īe** (*No [problem]*) and どういたしまして **Dō itashimashite** (*You're welcome*).

Apologizing

To apologize, say すみません **Sumimasen** or どうもすみません **Dōmo sumimasen**. You can also say a slightly informal version, ごめんなさい **Gomennasai**, to your family members or close friends.

To respond to apology, you can just respond with いいえ **Īe**, meaning *no need to apologize*, if the apology is for something not serious. If the apology is for something rather serious, you can respond to it with はい **hai**, meaning that you'll accept his/her apology.

EXERCISE
2·22

What would you say in Japanese in the following situations?

1. You accidentally pushed the person in front of you in a bus.

_____

2. Your neighbor brought homemade cake to your house.

_____

3. You are talking with your Japanese teacher and just realized that you forgot to do your homework that was due today.

_____

4. Your friend just thanked you for helping her carry the big package.

_____

5. Your friend just stepped on your foot and apologized to you.

_____

EXERCISE
2·23

George accidentally stepped on a woman's foot in a bus. Read their dialog and choose the appropriate answer from the options in parentheses.

GEORGE   あ, すみません。

        A, sumimasen.

A WOMAN   (はい, いいえ)。

        (Hai, Īe).

GEORGE   だいじょうぶですか。

        Daijōbu desu ka.

A WOMAN   はい, だいじょうぶです。

        Hai, daijōbu desu.

(だいじょうぶ **daijōbu** means *all right*)

EXERCISE
2·24

George forgot to do his homework and apologizes to his teacher. Read their dialog and choose the appropriate answer from the options in parentheses.

GEORGE 先生, どうもすみません。

Sensei, dōmo sumimasen.

TEACHER (はい, いいえ)。気をつけてくださいね。

(Hai, Īe). Ki o tsukete kudasai ne.

GEORGE はい。

Hai.

(気をつけてくださいね。 **Ki o tsukete kudasai ne.** means *Be careful, okay?*)

Referring to things around you

You can refer to things you and your conversation partner can see by using demonstrative adjectives along with a common noun such as 本 **hon** (*book*) or by using a demonstrative pronoun such as これ **kore** (*this one*), それ **sore** (*that one near you*), or あれ **are** (*that one over there*).

Demonstrative adjectives

When referring to an item that is close to you, use この **kono**, as in この本 **kono hon** (*this book*). If it is not close to you but close to your conversation partner, use その **sono**, as in その本 **sono hon** (*that book near you*). If far from both you and your conversation partner, use あの **ano**, as in あの本 **ano hon** (*that book over there*).

Things around you

The following are some common nouns for things around you:

book	本	**hon**
bag	かばん	**kaban**
camera	カメラ	**kamera**
car	車	**kuruma**
cell phone	携帯	**keitai**
chair	椅子	**isu**
computer, PC	パソコン	**pasokon**
desk	机	**tsukue**
eyeglasses	めがね	**megane**
key	鍵	**kagi**
notebook	ノート	**nōto**
pen	ペン	**pen**
sunglasses	サングラス	**sangurasu**
umbrella	傘	**kasa**
wallet	財布	**saifu**

Demonstrative pronouns これ **kore**, それ **sore**, and あれ **are**

When your conversation partner will know what noun you're referring to, you don't have to say the common noun but can use demonstrative pronouns, これ **kore** (*this one*), それ **sore** (*that one near you*), and あれ **are** (*that one over there*) except when you're referring to people.

When referring to people, do not use demonstrative pronouns but always use a demonstrative adjective along with a common noun—for example, あの人 **ano hito** (*that person over there*). To make it sound polite, you can use 方 **kata** to mean *person*, after a demonstrative adjective. For example:

> あの方は田中先生です。
> **Ano kata wa Tanaka sensei desu.**
> *That person over there is Professor Tanaka.*

For each of the following, choose the correct answer from the options in parentheses.

1. (あれ, あの)は谷さんのかばんです。

   (Are, Ano) wa Tani-san no kaban desu.

2. (これ, この)車はドイツの車です。

   (Kore, Kono) kuruma wa Doitsu no kuruma desu.

3. 私のパソコンは(それ, その)です。

   Watashi no pasokon wa (sore, sono) desu.

4. (あの人, あれ)は田中さんです。

   (Ano hito, Are) wa Tanaka-san desu.

For each of the following, choose the correct answer from the options in parentheses.

1. 鍵 **kagi**	(*wallet, key, umbrella*)
2. 財布 **saifu**	(*wallet, key, umbrella*)
3. サングラス **sangurasu**	(*sandwich, eyeglasses, notebook, sunglasses*)
4. パソコン **pasokon**	(*computer, pen, camera, bread*)

Asking "which?" "what?" and "whose?"

Sometimes to determine what particular item someone is talking about, you need to ask questions using a question word like *which item*, *what item*, and *whose item*. Remember that question words cannot be marked by the topic particle は **wa**.

The question word どの **dono** or どれ **dore** (*which*)

When you want to ask *which* or *which one*, you can say どの **dono** or どれ **dore**, as in:

> どの本ですか。
> **Dono hon desu ka.**
> *Which book is it?*

どれですか。
Dore desu ka.
Which one is it?

Like この **kono**, その **sono**, and あの **ano**, どの **dono** must be followed by a noun.

The question word 何 nani/nan (*what*)

To ask *what*, use 何, which is read as **nani** by itself but as **nan** when followed by です **desu**, as in 何ですか **nan desu ka**. For example:

これは何ですか。
Kore wa nan desu ka.
What is this?

The question word だれの dare no (*whose*)

To ask *whose*, say だれの **dare no**, which is だれ **dare** plus the particle の **no**. After the particle の **no**, you can drop the common noun if understood. For example:

これはだれの本ですか。
Kore wa dare no hon desu ka.
Whose book is this?

これはだれのですか。
Kore wa dare no desu ka.
Whose is this?

EXERCISE 2·27

Translate the following short dialogues into English.

1. A: これはだれの傘ですか。

   Kore wa dare no kasa desu ka.

   _____

   B: それはケンさんの傘です。

   Sore wa Ken-san no kasa desu.

   _____

2. A: あれはだれのですか。

   Are wa dare no desu ka.

   _____

   B: あれはジェーンさんのです。

   Are wa Jēn-san no desu.

   _____

3. A: あの車はだれの車ですか。

   Ano kuruma wa dare no kuruma desu ka.

   _____

B: あれは田中さんのです。

Are wa Tanaka-san no desu.

---

4. A: スミスさんのはどれですか。

Sumisu-san no wa dore desu ka.

B: あれです。

Are desu.

---

5. A: あの車は何ですか。

Ano kuruma wa nan desu ka.

B: あれはトヨタのカローラです。

Are wa Toyota no Karōra desu.

EXERCISE
2·28

For each of the following, choose the correct answer from the options in parentheses.

1. (これ, この) 車は日本の車です。

   (Kore, Kono) kuruma wa Nihon no kuruma desu.

2. 私のは (それ, その) です。

   Watashi no wa (sore, sono) desu.

3. A: それは何ですか。

   Sore wa nan desu ka.

   B: (これ, それ) はカメラです。

   (Kore, sore) wa kamera desu.

4. あの人は (だれ, 何) ですか。

   Ano hito wa (dare, nan) desu ka.

5. これは (だれ, 何) ですか。

   Kore wa (dare, nan) desu ka.

6. それは (山田さん, 山田さんの) ですか。

   Sore wa (Yamada-san, Yamada-san no) desu ka.

Reorder the items in each set to create a grammatical sentence.

1. 本 **hon**, 父 **chichi**, あれ **are**, の **no**, は **wa**, です **desu**

   _____

2. これ **kore**, です **desu**, 私 **watashi**, は **wa**, の **no**

   _____

3. だれ **dare**, あの **ano**, 学生 **gakusei**, か **ka**, は **wa**, です **desu**

   _____

4. 何 **nan**, それ **sore**, は **wa**, です **desu**, か **ka**

   _____

5. ケンさん **Ken-san**, どれ **dore**, は **wa**, です **desu**, か **ka**, の **no**

   _____

One rainy day, many umbrellas are in the classroom. Yukiko and George are trying to figure out which one is whose. Complete their conversation as appropriate.

YUKIKO   ジョージさん。これはジョージさんの傘ですか。

         Jōji-san. Kore wa Jōji-san no kasa desu ka.

GEORGE   いいえ, 僕のじゃありません。田中さんのです。

         Īe, boku no ja arimasen. Tanaka-san no desu.

YUKIKO   ああ, そうですか。

         Ā, sō desu ka.

GEORGE   僕のはこれです。雪子さんのは _____ ですか。

         Boku no wa kore desu. Yukiko-san no wa _____ desu ka.

YUKIKO   私のはあれです。

         Watashi no wa are desu.

GEORGE   じゃあ, それはだれの傘ですか。

         Jā, sore wa dare no kasa desu ka.

YUKIKO   _____ は奈々子さんのです。

         _____ wa Nanako-san no desu.

·3· Using numbers

This chapter introduces Japanese number systems and many situations where you need to use numbers. You will learn how to speak about time-related concepts, such as ages, calendar dates, and holidays. You will also learn how to ask and answer questions such as "how much?" and "how many?"

Numbers from 1 to 10

There are two number systems in Japanese: the Chinese system and the native Japanese system. The native Japanese system is a native numeral plus the native counter つ **tsu**. It is frequently used, and it only goes up to 10 in modern Japanese.

The Chinese system is predominantly used in business/administrative/academic contexts. However, **shi** (*four*) and **shichi** (*seven*) in the Chinese system are often replaced by **yon** and **nana** in the native Japanese system. In fact, **shi**, **shichi**, and **ku** (a variation of **kyū**) are used only in reciting numerals, such as when quickly counting or doing physical exercises.

Numbers are written as Arabic numerals most of the time in business/administrative/academic contexts, but they may be written in kanji. The following table shows the Arabic numeral, the kanji, the pronunciation in the Chinese system, and the pronunciation in the native Japanese system for the numbers 1 through 10:

Arabic Numeral	Kanji	Chinese System	Native Japanese System
1	一	いち **ichi**	ひとつ **hitotsu**
2	二	に **ni**	ふたつ **futatsu**
3	三	さん **san**	みっつ **mittsu**
4	四	し **shi** (or よん **yon**)	よっつ **yottsu**
5	五	ご **go**	いつつ **itsutsu**
6	六	ろく **roku**	むっつ **muttsu**
7	七	しち **shichi** (or なな **nana**)	ななつ **nanatsu**
8	八	はち **hachi**	やっつ **yattsu**
9	九	きゅう **kyū** (or く **ku**)	ここのつ **kokonotsu**
10	十	じゅう **jū**	とお **tō**

Read the sequence of the numbers in the Chinese system from 1 to 10 until you memorize it.

いち, に, さん, し, ご, ろく, しち, はち, きゅう, じゅう
ichi, ni, san, shi, go, roku, shichi, hachi, kyū, jū

EXERCISE
3·2

Read the sequence of the numbers in the native Japanese system from 1 to 10 until you memorize it.

ひとつ, ふたつ, みっつ, よっつ, いつつ, むっつ, ななつ, やっつ, ここのつ, とお
hitotsu, futatsu, mittsu yottsu, itsutsu, muttsu, nanatsu, yattsu, kokonotsu, tō

EXERCISE
3·3

What is your favorite number? Say it in Japanese in the two systems.

Numbers from 11 to 99

The native Japanese number system goes only through 10 in modern Japanese, so beyond that, Japanese use the Chinese system. In the Chinese system, the numbers from 11 to 19 are compound words consisting of **jū** (*ten*) plus one of the other digits. For example, 12 is **jū-ni**. The even tens (*twenty, thirty, forty*, etc.) are compound words consisting of one of the numbers plus **jū** (*ten*). For example, 20 is **ni-jū**. Beyond 20, you use the word for the even ten plus the other digit. As you would expect, 23 is **ni-jū-san**, and 99 is **kyū-jū-kyū**.

EXERCISE
3·4

Read the sequence of the numbers from 11 to 20 aloud.

じゅういち, じゅうに, じゅうさん, じゅうし, じゅうご, じゅうろく, じゅうしち, じゅうはち, じゅうく, にじゅう
jū-ichi, jū-ni, jū-san, jū-shi, jū-go, jū-roku, jū-shichi, jū-hachi, jū-ku, ni-jū

Note: Alternative pronunciations for 14, 17, and 19 are じゅうよん **jū-yon**, じゅうなな **jū-nana**, and じゅうきゅう **jū-kyū**.

Write the following numbers in hiragana or romaji.

1. 15 _____

2. 38 _____

3. 56 _____

4. 77 _____

5. 89 _____

Numbers from 100 to 99,999

The following table shows the multiples of 100, 1,000, and 10,000. Notice some sound changes with the multiples of 100 (**hyaku, byaku,** and **pyaku**) and 1,000 (**sen** and **zen**).

100	ひゃく **hyaku**	1,000	せん **sen**	10,000	いちまん **ichi-man**
200	にひゃく **ni-hyaku**	2,000	にせん **ni-sen**	20,000	にまん **ni-man**
300	さんびゃく **san-byaku**	3,000	さんぜん **san-zen**	30,000	さんまん **san-man**
400	よんひゃく **yon-hyaku**	4,000	よんせん **yon-sen**	40,000	よんまん **yon-man**
500	ごひゃく **go-hyaku**	5,000	ごせん **go-sen**	50,000	ごまん **go-man**
600	ろっぴゃく **rop-pyaku**	6,000	ろくせん **roku-sen**	60,000	ろくまん **roku-man**
700	ななひゃく **nana-hyaku**	7,000	ななせん **nana-sen**	70,000	ななまん **nana-man**
800	はっぴゃく **hap-pyaku**	8,000	はっせん **has-sen**	80,000	はちまん **hachi-man**
900	きゅうひゃく **kyū-hyaku**	9,000	きゅうせん **kyū-sen**	90,000	きゅうまん **kyū-man**

EXERCISE
3·6

Write the following numbers in hiragana or romaji and then pronounce them a few times each.

1. 22,222 _____

2. 33,333 _____

3. 66,666 _____

4. 88,888 _____

5. 99,999 _____

EXERCISE
3·7

Write the following numbers in hiragana or romaji.

1. 19,800 _____

2. 44,771 _____

3. 56,525 _____

Expressing age with the counter 歳 sai

To express a person's age, you add 歳 **sai** after the numeral in the Chinese system. For example, 15 歳 **jū-go-sai** means *15 years old*. You can express the age of a young child by using the native Japanese system also. For example, みっつ **mittsu** means *3 years old*. To ask someone his age, say 何歳ですか **Nan-sai desu ka** (*How old are you?*). For elderly people, you can ask おいくつですか **O-ikutsu desu ka** (*How old are you?*) to sound polite. When **sai** is combined with certain numerals, it causes some sound change, as you can see:

1 歳	2 歳	3 歳	4 歳	5 歳	6 歳	7 歳	8 歳	9 歳	10 歳
いっさい	にさい	さんさい	よんさい	ごさい	ろくさい	ななさい	はっさい	きゅうさい	じゅっさい or じっさい
is-sai	ni-sai	san-sai	yon-sai	go-sai	roku-sai	nana-sai	has-sai	kyū-sai	jus-sai or jis-sai

EXERCISE
3·8

Read the previous table three times aloud.

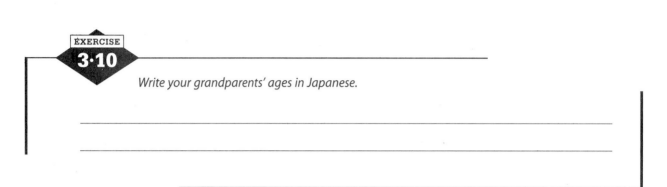

EXERCISE
3·9

How old are you? Say it in Japanese.

EXERCISE
3·10

Write your grandparents' ages in Japanese.

_____

_____

Telephone numbers

The word for *telephone number* is 電話番号 **denwa-bangō**. Telephone numbers are expressed using the Chinese number system. However, use れい **rei** or ゼロ **zero** (from the English word *zero*) for *zero*. Use よん **yon** for *four* and なな **nana** for *seven*. To ask someone's telephone number, say the person's name and add の電話番号は何ですか **no denwa-bangō wa nan desu ka**. For example:

> 山田さんの電話番号は何ですか。
> **Yamada-san no denwa-bangō wa nan desu ka.**
> *What is your phone number, Ms. Yamada?*

For asking someone else's phone number, you can use わかりますか **wakarimasu ka** at the end, as in:

> 吉川さんの電話番号はわかりますか。
> **Yoshikawa-san no denwa-bangō wa wakarimasu ka.**
> *Do you know Mr. Yoshikawa's telephone number?*

EXERCISE
3·11

Read the following sentences aloud, paying attention to the pronunciation of the telephone numbers.

1. 東京の山田さんの電話番号は 03-5272-4353 です。

   Tōkyō no Yamada-san no denwa-bangō wa zero-san go-ni-nana-ni yon-san-go-san desu.

2. 大阪の石田さんの電話番号は 06-6459-1507 です。

   Ōsaka no Ishida-san no denwa-bangō wa zero-roku roku-yon-go-kyū ichi-go-zero-nana desu.

3. 名古屋の大川さんの電話番号は 052-459-0281 です。

Nagoya no Ōkawa-san no denwa-bangō wa zero-go-ni yon-go-kyū zero-ni-hachi-ichi desu.

EXERCISE

3·12

Write your telephone number in Arabic numerals and say it in Japanese 10 times.

EXERCISE

3·13

Write the cell phone numbers of your family members in Arabic numerals and say them three times each in Japanese.

EXERCISE

3·14

Jerry asks Yukiko some questions. Read their conversation and indicate what the underlined parts mean.

JERRY   すみません。雪子さんの電話番号は何ですか。

Sumimasen. Yukiko-san no denwa-bangō wa nan desu ka.

YUKIKO   携帯は 918-332-3322 です。うちは 052-555-7766 です。

Keitai wa kyū-ichi-hachi san-san-ni san-san-ni-ni desu. Uchi wa zero-go-ni go-go-go nana-nana-roku-roku desu.

JERRY   ああ, そうですか。どうも。

Ā, sō desu ka. Dōmo.

それから順子さんの電話番号はわかりますか。

Sorekara Junko-san no denwa-bangō wa wakarimasu ka.

YUKIKO	1. ちょっとわかりません。
	1. Chotto wakarimasen.
JERRY	ああ, そうですか。2. じゃあ, いいです。
	Ā, sō desu ka. 2. Jā, ii desu.

1. _____

2. _____

Telling time

Time-related expressions include absolute time expressions that specify the time that you can point at on a calendar or on a clock—for example, *June 2, 4 PM*, etc.—and relative time expressions, such as *now, tomorrow,* and *last month.* In addition, Japanese has many words that refer to specific time periods in a day.

Counters for time: 時 ji and 分 fun

The following list shows how time is expressed in Japanese. Pay special attention to irregular pronunciations.

1時 **ichi-ji** *1 o'clock*	1分 **ip-pun** *1 minute*	
2時 **ni-ji** *2 o'clock*	2分 **ni-fun** *2 minutes*	
3時 **san-ji** *3 o'clock*	3分 **san-pun** *3 minutes*	
4時 **yo-ji** *4 o'clock*	4分 **yon-pun** *4 minutes*	
5時 **go-ji** *5 o'clock*	5分 **go-fun** *5 minutes*	
6時 **roku-ji** *6 o'clock*	6分 **rop-pun** *6 minutes*	
7時 **shichi-ji** *7 o'clock*	7分 **nana-fun** *7 minutes*	
8時 **hachi-ji** *8 o'clock*	8分 **hap-pun** (**hachi-fun**) *8 minutes*	
9時 **ku-ji** *9 o'clock*	9分 **kyū-fun** *9 minutes*	
10時 **jū-ji** *10 o'clock*	10分 **jup-pun** (**jip-pun**) *10 minutes*	
11時 **jū-ichi-ji** *11 o'clock*	15分 **jū-go-fun** *15 minutes*	
12時 **jū-ni-ji** *12 o'clock*	30分 **san-jup-pun** *30 minutes*	

Add 午前 **gozen** (AM) and 午後 **gogo** (PM) before the time phrase. A half an hour (30 minutes) can be expressed by 半 **han**. For example:

午前2時15分 **gozen ni-ji jū-go-fun** (*2:15 AM*)
午後3時30分 **gogo san-ji san-jup-pun** (*3:30 PM*)
午前2時半 **gozen ni-ji han** (*2:30 AM*)

Use the particle に **ni** after a time phrase to express the time of an event. For example:

7時におきました。
Shichi-ji ni okimashita.
I woke up at 7 AM.

Relative time expressions

You use relative time expressions to specify time relative to the current moment, such as *tomorrow* or *last year.* The following list shows some common relative time expressions:

last month	先月	**sengetsu**
last week	先週	**senshū**

last year	去年	kyonen
next month	来月	raigetsu
next week	来週	raishū
next year	来年	rainen
now	今	ima
this month	今月	kongetsu
this morning	今朝	kesa
this week	今週	konshū
this year	今年	kotoshi
today	今日	kyō
tomorrow	あした／明日	ashita/asu (myōnichi)
tonight	今晩	konban
yesterday	昨日	kinō/sakujitsu

Daily time frames

Based on the combination of the absolute time and the position of the sun, a day can be divided into at least eight time frames, as shown in the following list. Here you can see that 午後 **gogo** can mean both *PM* and *afternoon*.

A few hours before sunrise	明け方	**akegata**
A few hours after sunrise	朝	**asa**
Between a few hours after sunrise and noon	午前中	**gozenchū**
From noon to 1 PM	昼	**hiru**
Between 1 PM and a few hours before sunset	午後	**gogo**
A few hours before sunset	夕方	**yūgata**
After sunset and before midnight	晩	**ban**
After midnight and before sunrise	真夜中	**mayonaka**

EXERCISE
3·15

Complete the following dialog between Mike and a stranger at a train station.

MIKE すみません。今, 1. _____ ですか。

Sumimasen. Ima, 1. _____ **desu ka.**

Excuse me. What time it is now?

A MAN 今, 2時25分です。

Ima, ni-ji ni-jū-go-fun desu.

It's 2:25 now.

MIKE ああ, そうですか。2. _____ 。

Ā, sō desu ka. 2. _____ .

Oh, I see. Thank you.

A MAN いいえ。

Īe.

No problem.

Complete the conversation between Akiko and Takeshi.

AKIKO   武さん。今日は 1. _____ おきましたか。

Takeshi-san. Kyō wa 1. _____ okimashita ka.

Takeshi. What time did you wake up today?

TAKESHI   今日は 2. _____ おきました。

Kyō wa 2. _____ okimashita.

I woke up at 8 o'clock today.

Mr. Tanaka is going to Boston tomorrow for a conference. Complete the conversation between him and Ms. Ueda.

MS. UEDA   田中さん。あしたのボストンへの飛行機は何時ですか。

Tanaka-san. Ashita no Boston e no hikōki wa nan-ji desu ka.

What time is the flight for Boston tomorrow, Mr. Tanaka?

MR. TANAKA   1. _____ です。

1. _____ **desu.**

It's at 6:35 AM.

MS. UEDA   ああ, そうですか。会議は何時からですか。

Ā, sō desu ka. Kaigi wa nan-ji kara desu ka.

Oh, I see. What time will the conference start?

MR. TANAKA   2. _____ からです。

2. _____ **kara desu.**

It starts at 1 PM.

MS. UEDA   ああ, そうですか。

Ā, sō desu ka.

Oh, I see.

MR. TANAKA   夕方にはニューヨークに戻ります。

Yūgata ni wa Nyū Yōku ni modorimasu.

I'll return to New York by early evening.

The calendar

To refer to a specific day, you can combine the name of the day in a week, the name of the month, the name of the date in the month, and the name of the year. Unlike in English, the names of months include numerals in Japanese. This section shows you how to combine these names to refer to a specific day in Japanese.

Days of the week

The following list shows how to express the days of the week in Japanese:

Sunday	日曜日	**Nichiyōbi**
Monday	月曜日	**Getsuyōbi**
Tuesday	火曜日	**Kayōbi**
Wednesday	水曜日	**Suiyōbi**
Thursday	木曜日	**Mokuyōbi**
Friday	金曜日	**Kinyōbi**
Saturday	土曜日	**Doyōbi**

Months

The following list shows how to express the months in Japanese:

January	1月	**Ichi-gatsu**
February	2月	**Ni-gatsu**
March	3月	**San-gatsu**
April	4月	**Shi-gatsu**
May	5月	**Go-gatsu**
June	6月	**Roku-gatsu**
July	7月	**Shichi-gatsu**
August	8月	**Hachi-gatsu**
September	9月	**Ku-gatsu**
October	10月	**Jū-gatsu**
November	11月	**Jūichi-gatsu**
December	12月	**Jūni-gatsu**

Days of the month

The days of the month are very difficult to learn because the first 10 days are not systematic. As the following list shows, most of the days after the 10th follow an easily learned pattern:

1st	1日	**tsuitachi**
2nd	2日	**futsuka**
3rd	3日	**mikka**
4th	4日	**yokka**
5th	5日	**itsuka**
6th	6日	**muika**
7th	7日	**nanoka**
8th	8日	**yōka**
9th	9日	**kokonoka**
10th	10日	**tōka**
11th	11日	**jūichi-nichi**
12th	12日	**jūni-nichi**
13th	13日	**jūsan-nichi**
14th	14日	**jūyokka**
15th	15日	**jūgo-nichi**

16th	16日	**jūroku-nichi**
17th	17日	**jūshichi-nichi**
18th	18日	**jūhachi-nichi**
19th	19日	**jūku-nichi**
20th	20日	**hatsuka**
21st	21日	**nijū ichi-nichi**
22nd	22日	**nijū ni-nichi**
23rd	23日	**nijū san-nichi**
24th	24日	**nijū yokka**
25th	25日	**nijū go-nichi**
26th	26日	**nijū roku-nichi**
27th	27日	**nijū shichi-nichi**
28th	28日	**nijū hachi-nichi**
29th	29日	**nijū ku-nichi**
30th	30日	**sanjū-nichi**
31st	31日	**sanjūichi-nichi**

Years are expressed using the Western system, with the counter 年 **-nen**, as in 2013年 **ni-sen-jū-san-nen** (*2013*), or using the Japanese system, with 年号 **nengō** (*era name*) and the counter **-nen**, as in 平成25年 **Heisei ni-jū-go-nen** (*Heisei 25, 2013*). A new **nengō** is created every time a new emperor ascends the throne in Japan and continues to be used until a different emperor takes his place. For example, a date can be written as:

2013年12月14日 土曜日
(Pronunciation: **ni-sen-jū-san-nen jū-ni-gatsu jū-yokka Doyōbi**)
Saturday, December 14th, 2013

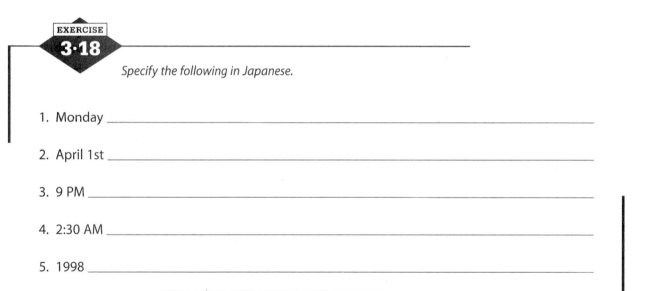

EXERCISE
3·18

Specify the following in Japanese.

1. Monday _____

2. April 1st _____

3. 9 PM _____

4. 2:30 AM _____

5. 1998 _____

Asking "when?"

Here you'll learn how to ask "when?" appropriately depending on the context. You'll also learn major Japanese holidays.

Question word いつ itsu (*when*)

Use いつ **itsu** to ask "when?" You do not need to place a particle after いつ **itsu**. However, to ask more specific question, you can use expressions like 何時 **nan-ji** (*what o'clock*), 何分 **nan-pun** (*what minute*), 何曜日 **nan-yōbi** (*what day of a week*), 何月 **nan-gatsu** (*what month*), 何年 **nan-nen** (*what year*), 何日 **nan-nichi** (*what date*), etc., along with the particle に **ni**.

For example:

今、何時ですか。
Ima nan-ji desu ka.
What time is it now?

今日は何曜日ですか。
Kyō wa nan-yōbi desu ka.
What day is it today?

Japanese national holidays

The following table lists some of Japan's national holidays. Can you state which date each of the national holiday is in Japanese?

English Translation	Date	Japanese	Romaji
New Year's Day	1月1日	元日	**Ganjitsu**
Coming-of-Age Day	Second Monday of January	成人の日	**Seijin no hi**
National Foundation Day	2月11日	建国記念日	**Kenkoku-kinen-bi**
Emperor's Birthday	2月23日	天皇誕生日	**Tennō tanjōbi**
Vernal Equinox Day	Around 3月20日	春分の日	**Shunbun no hi**
Showa Day	4月29日	昭和の日	**Shōwa no hi**
Constitution Memorial Day	5月3日	憲法記念日	**Kenpō kinenbi**
Greenery Day	5月4日	緑の日	**Midori no hi**
Children's Day	5月5日	こどもの日	**Kodomo no hi**
Ocean Day	Third Monday of July	海の日	**Umi no hi**
Mountain Day	8月11日	山の日	**Yama no hi**
Respect-for-the-Aged Day	Third Monday of September	敬老の日	**Keirō no hi**
Autumnal Equinox Day	Around 9月23日	秋分の日	**Shūbun no hi**
Sports Day	Second Monday of October	スポーツの日	**Supōtsu no hi**
Culture Day	11月3日	文化の日	**Bunka no hi**
Labor Thanksgiving Day	11月23日	勤労感謝の日	**Kinrō-kansha no hi**

Answer the following questions in Japanese.

1. 子どもの日はいつですか。

   Kodomo no hi wa itsu desu ka.

   When is the Children's Day?

   _____

2. バレンタインデーはいつですか。

   Barentain Dē wa itsu desu ka.

   When is Valentine's Day?

   _____

Answer the following questions in Japanese based on the fact.

1. 今, 何月ですか。

   Ima, nan-gatsu desu ka.

   What month is it now?

   _____

2. 先月は何月でしたか。

   Sengetsu wa nan-gatsu deshita ka.

   What month was it last month?

   _____

3. 来月は何月ですか。

   Raigetsu wa nan-gatsu desu ka.

   What month is it next month?

   _____

4. 今日は何月何日ですか。

   Kyō wa nan-gatsu nan-nichi desu ka.

   What month and date is it today?

   _____

5. あしたは何日ですか。

   Ashita wa nan-nichi desu ka.

   What date is it tomorrow?

   _____

EXERCISE
3·21

Answer the following questions about yourself in Japanese.

1. 何年に生まれましたか。

   Nan-nen ni umaremashita ka.

   Which year were you born in?

   _____

2. 誕生日はいつですか。

   Tanjōbi wa itsu desu ka.

   When is your birthday?

   _____

Asking "how much?" at a store

When you want to purchase something in a store, you need to know how to ask "how much?" along with the name of the item you want. You also need to know how to say which item or items you would like to purchase.

Things you might buy at an electronics store

Examine the following list of goods you might purchase at an electronics store:

watch/clock	時計	**tokei**
necklace	ネックレス	**nekkuresu**
computer	パソコン	**pasokon**
cell phone	携帯 (電話)	**keitai (denwa)**
smart phone	スマートフォン	**sumātofon**
printer	プリンター	**purintā**
camera	カメラ	**kamera**
game software	ゲームソフト	**gēmusofuto**
scanner	スキャナー	**sukyanā**
tablet	タブレット	**taburetto**

Asking "how much?" with いくら **ikura**

Use いくら **ikura** to ask the price of something. For example:

> あのカメラはいくらですか。
> **Ano kamera wa ikura desu ka.**
> *How much is that camera?*

You can also use 何ドルですか **Nan-doru desu ka** (*How much in dollars?*) or 何円ですか **Nan-en desu ka** (*How much in Japanese yen?*) if currency units need to be clarified.

Shopping by saying . . . をください o kudasai

Once you decide to buy something, say the name of the item and add をください **o kudasai**. It means *Please give it to me*, and is a perfect phrase to let the store clerk know what you decided to buy. For example:

あの時計をください。
Ano tokei o kudasai.
I'll take that watch.

Listing nouns with と to

If you are buying multiple items, connect them with the particle と **to**. For example:

このパソコンとこのスキャナーとあのプリンターをください。
Kono pasokon to kono sukyanā to ano purintā o kudasai.
May I have this PC, this scanner, and that printer?

EXERCISE
3·22

Kazuko is trying to buy a wrist watch at a store in Japan. Complete the following conversation appropriately.

KAZUKO   すみません。その時計はいくらですか。

    Sumimasen. Sono tokei wa ikura desu ka.

    Excuse me. How much is that watch?

STORE CLERK   これですか。

    Kore desu ka.

    This one?

KAZUKO   はい。

    Hai.

    Yes.

STORE CLERK   これは12,000円です。

    Kore wa ichi-man-ni-sen-en desu.

    This one is 12,000 yen.

KAZUKO   ああ, そうですか。じゃあ, あの時計は 1.＿＿＿＿＿＿＿＿＿ ですか。

    Ā, sō desu ka. Jā, ano tokei wa 1.＿＿＿＿＿＿ desu ka.

    Oh, I see. Then, how much is that watch?

STORE CLERK   あれは1,500円です。

    Are wa sen-go-hyaku-en desu.

    That one is 1,500 yen.

KAZUKO	じゃあ, この時計とあの時計を 2. _____。
	Jā, kono tokei to ano tokei o 2. _____.
	Then, please give me this watch and that watch.
STORE CLERK	ありがとうございます。
	Arigatō gozaimasu.
	Thank you very much.

Asking "how many?" with counters

Japanese uses different counters to express the amount or quantity of a variety of items. The choice of counters varies depending on the shapes, sizes, and types of items. When you ask "how many?" you need to use a number phrase that is made of a numeral and the appropriate counter.

Using number phrases in a sentence

You need to place a counter after the numeral whenever you want to express the quantity or amount of virtually anything—whether it's people, animals, or cars. The choice of counters varies depending on the shape, size, and type of the item. For example, if there are two sheets of origami paper, you say 折り紙が2枚あります **Origami ga ni-mai arimasu**. If there are two pens, you say ペンが2本あります **Pen ga ni-hon arimasu**. To express existence or to mean *there is . . .* or *there are . . .*, あります **arimasu** is used for inanimate items, and います **imasu** is used for animate items. See Chapter 6 for these existential verbs.

Frequently used counters

The following are some frequently used counters:

cylindrical-shaped objects (e.g., bananas, pens, pencils, cigarettes, bottles)	本 **hon/bon/pon**
flat-shaped objects (e.g., paper, sheets, tickets, postal stamps)	枚 **mai**
mechanical objects (e.g., TV, radio, computer, refrigerator)	台 **dai**
small or medium-size animals (e.g., fish, dogs, cats)	匹 **hiki/biki/piki**
bound items (e.g., books, dictionaries, notebooks, magazines)	冊 **satsu**
people (e.g., students, children); a native number phrase is used for one (1) and two (2)	人 **nin**
a variety of inanimate items (e.g., chairs, beds, apples, candies); used with Japanese native numerals	つ **tsu**

Some of these counters cause irregular sound changes. The pronunciations of the counters with numerals from 1 to 10 are as follows. Notice that the pronunciation し **shi** for the number 4 is rarely used when combined with a counter.

The following tables show how different counters are pronounced when they are combined with numerals:

COUNTING LONG ITEMS

1本 (一本)	2本 (二本)	3本 (三本)	4本 (四本)	5本 (五本)	6本 (六本)	7本 (七本)	8本 (八本)	9本 (九本)	10本 (十本)
いっぽん	にほん	さんぼん	よんほん	ごほん	ろっぽん	ななほん	はっぽん	きゅうほん	じゅっぽん/じっぽん
ip-pon	ni-hon	san-bon	yon-hon	go-hon	rop-pon	nana-hon	hap-pon	kyū-hon	jup-pon/jip-pon

COUNTING FLAT ITEMS

1枚 (一枚)	2枚 (二枚)	3枚 (三枚)	4枚 (四枚)	5枚 (五枚)	6枚 (六枚)	7枚 (七枚)	8枚 (八枚)	9枚 (九枚)	10枚 (十枚)
いちまい	にまい	さんまい	よんまい	ごまい	ろくまい	ななまい	はちまい	きゅうまい	じゅうまい
ichi-mai	ni-mai	san-mai	yon-mai	go-mai	roku-mai	nana-mai	hachi-mai	kyū-mai	jū-mai

COUNTING MACHINES

1台 (一台)	2台 (二台)	3台 (三台)	4台 (四台)	5台 (五台)	6台 (六台)	7台 (七台)	8台 (八台)	9台 (九台)	10台 (十台)
いちだい	にだい	さんだい	よんだい	ごだい	ろくだい	ななだい	はちだい	きゅうだい	じゅうだい
ichi-dai	ni-dai	san-dai	yon-dai	go-dai	roku-dai	nana-dai	hachi-dai	kyū-dai	jū-dai

COUNTING SMALL OR MEDIUM-SIZE ANIMALS

1匹 (一匹)	2匹 (二匹)	3匹 (三匹)	4匹 (四匹)	5匹 (五匹)	6匹 (六匹)	7匹 (七匹)	8匹 (八匹)	9匹 (九匹)	10匹 (十匹)
いっぴき	にひき	さんびき	よんひき	ごひき	ろっぴき	ななひき	はっぴき	きゅうひき	じゅっぴき / じっぴき
ip-piki	ni-hiki	san-biki	yon-hiki	go-hiki	rop-piki	nana-hiki	hap-piki	kyū-hiki	jup-piki/jip-piki

COUNTING BOUND ITEMS

1冊 (一冊)	2冊 (二冊)	3冊 (三冊)	4冊 (四冊)	5冊 (五冊)	6冊 (六冊)	7冊 (七冊)	8冊 (八冊)	9冊 (九冊)	10冊 (十冊)
いっさつ	にさつ	さんさつ	よんさつ	ごさつ	ろくさつ	ななさつ	はっさつ	きゅうさつ	じゅっさつ / じっさつ
is-satsu	ni-satsu	san-satsu	yon-satsu	go-satsu	roku-satsu	nana-satsu	has-satsu	kyū-satsu	jus-satsu/jis-satsu

COUNTING PEOPLE

1人 (一人)	2人 (二人)	3人 (三人)	4人 (四人)	5人 (五人)	6人 (六人)	7人 (七人)	8人 (八人)	9人 (九人)	10人 (十人)
ひと り	ふた り	さんに ん	よに ん	ごにん	ろくに ん	ななにん / しちにん	はちに ん	きゅうに ん	じゅうに ん
hito-ri	futa-ri	san-nin	yo-nin	go-nin	roku- nin	nana-nin/ shichi-nin	hachi- nin	kyū-nin	jū-nin

COUNTING MEDIUM-SIZE INANIMATE ITEMS

1つ (一つ)	2つ (二つ)	3つ (三つ)	4つ (四つ)	5つ (五つ)	6つ (六 つ)	7つ (七 つ)	8つ (八つ)	9つ (九つ)	10(十)
ひと つ	ふた つ	みっ つ	よっ つ	いつ つ	むっ つ	なな つ	やっ つ	ここの つ	とお
hito-tsu	futa-tsu	mit-tsu	yot-tsu	itsu-tsu	mut- tsu	nana- tsu	yat-tsu	kokono- tsu	tō

The most neutral way of expressing the amount or the quantity of some item in a sentence is to place a number phrase after the item you are counting along with the associated particle. For example:

切手が3枚あります。
Kitte ga san-mai arimasu.
There are three postage stamps.

切手を3枚ください。
Kitte o san-mai kudadai.
Please give me three stamps.

You can list multiple items in a sentence along with number phrases, as shown here:

100 円の切手が3枚と, 120円の切手が2枚あります。
Hyaku-en no kitte ga san-mai to, hyaku-ni-jū-en no kitte ga ni-mai arimasu.
There are three 100-yen stamps and two 120-yen stamps.

100 円の切手を3枚と, 120円の切手を2枚ください。
Hyaku-en no kitte o san-mai to hyaku-ni-jū-en no kitte o ni-mai kudasai.
Please give me three 100-yen stamps and two 120-yen stamps.

EXERCISE
3·23

Write the pronunciation of the following phrases in hiragana or romaji.

EXAMPLE   *Five origami sheets:* ごまい **go-mai** (5枚)

1. *Two students:* _____

2. *Three machines:* _____

3. *Two apples:* _____

4. *Five books:* _____

5. *Three cats:* _____

6. *One dog:* _____

Translate the following sentences into Japanese.

1. *There are two dogs.* (犬 **inu** means *dog*)

   _____

2. *There are four postage stamps.* (切手 **kitte** means *postage stamp*)

   _____

3. *There are three cars.* (車 **kuruma** means *car*)

   _____

4. *Please give me three notebooks.* (ノート **nōto** means *notebook*)

   _____

5. *Please give me two bananas.* (バナナ **banana** means *banana*)

   _____

6. *Please give me two bananas and three apples.* (りんご **ringo** means *apple*)

   _____

Around town

This chapter explains the basic verb conjugation system and shows you different way of expressing and asking about actions such as coming and going. You'll also learn how to ask questions that inquire "anywhere?" and "where?" as well as how to reply to such questions.

Basic verb forms and verb classes

Unlike English verbs, Japanese verbs do not change their forms based on person, gender, or number, but they change their forms based on the formality of speech (plain or polite), polarity (affirmative or negative), and tense (non-past or past). Non-past tense is used to express future actions and habitual actions, or actions that have not yet started. Past tense is used to express past actions or actions that have completed. There are only two major irregular verbs, する **suru** (*do*) and 来る **kuru** (*come*), and all the rest are regular verbs. There are two kinds of regular verbs: **ru** verbs and **u** verbs.

Dictionary and **masu** forms of verbs

The dictionary form of a verb is the plain non-past affirmative form. It is the shortest verb form that can end a sentence. It is called "dictionary form" because it is used for listing verbs in dictionaries. The **masu** form of a verb is the polite non-past affirmative form. It is the polite version of the dictionary form. For example, the dictionary form of the verb *to eat* is 食べる **taberu**, whereas its **masu** form is 食べます **tabemasu**.

Ru and u verbs

変える **kaeru** and 帰る **kaeru** are homophones. They sound the same in their dictionary forms, but their meanings are different, as shown by their differing kanji. 変える **kaeru** means *to change* and 帰る **kaeru** means *to return*. Although their dictionary forms are the same, they conjugate differently. The **masu** form of 変える **kaeru** is 変えます **kaemasu**, and the **masu** form of 帰る **kaeru** is 帰ります **kaerimasu**. So, for some verbs, you drop the final **ru** in the dictionary form and add **masu** to get a **masu** form. However, for other verbs, you drop **u** (pronounce it as *oo* not as *yoo*) and add **imasu**. The verbs in which you have to drop **ru** are called *ru verbs* and those in which you have to drop **u** are called *u verbs*.

The following table lists representative **ru** verbs and **u** verbs as well as the two major irregular verbs in the dictionary form and **masu** form. To conjugate a verb, you find out its verb class (**ru** verb, **u** verb, or irregular verb) and check the ending of the dictionary form, and then you follow the pattern of one of the verbs in the following table:

Verb Class	Ending of the Dictionary Form		Dictionary Form (Plain non-past affirmative)	Masu Form (Polite non-past affirmative)
	Hiragana	Romaji		
Ru verb	…eる	…eru	かえる **kaeru** (*change*)	かえます **kaemasu**
	…iる	…iru	きる **kiru** (*wear*)	きます **kimasu**
U verb	…す	…su	はなす **hanasu** (*speak*)	はなします **hanashimasu**
	…く	…ku	かく **kaku** (*write*)	かきます **kakimasu**
	…ぐ	…gu	およぐ **oyogu** (*swim*)	およぎます **oyogimasu**
	…む	…mu	よむ **yomu** (*read*)	よみます **yomimasu**
	…ぬ	…nu	しぬ **shinu** (*die*)	しにます **shinimasu**
	…ぶ	…bu	とぶ **tobu** (*jump*)	とびます **tobimasu**
	…う	…vowel + u	かう **kau** (*buy*)	かいます **kaimasu**
	…る	…ru	きる **kiru** (*cut*)	きります **kirimasu**
	…つ	…tsu	まつ **matsu** (*wait*)	まちます **machimasu**
Irregular verb			くる **kuru** (*come*)	きます **kimasu**
			する **suru** (*do*)	します **shimasu**

If you can see that the verb class is ambiguous only if a verb ends in -**iru** or -**eru**, you are on the right track. If a verb does not end in -**iru** or -**eru**, you can trust that it's an **u** verb. If it ends in -**iru** or -**eru**, you need to remember which class the verb belongs to each time. In this book, verbs are specified for verb class *only if* they end in -**iru** or -**eru**.

EXERCISE
4·1

*Change the following verbs from the dictionary form to the **masu** form. You should know whether they are **ru** verbs or **u** verbs by looking at their endings.*

1. 取る **toru** (*take*) _____

2. 売る **uru** (*sell*) _____

3. 始まる **hajimaru** (*start*) _____

4. 作る **tsukuru** (*make*) _____

5. 読む **yomu** (*read*) _____

6. 飲む **nomu** (*drink*) _____

7. 買う **kau** (*buy*) _____

8. 書く **kaku** (*write*) _____

9. 泳ぐ **oyogu** (*swim*) _____

10. 運ぶ **hakobu** (*carry*) _____

11. 待つ **matsu** (*wait*) _____

12. 話す **hanasu** (*speak*) _____

EXERCISE

4·2

The following verbs are all **ru** *verbs in the dictionary form. Convert them to the* **masu** *form.*

1. 変える **kaeru** (*change*) _____

2. 着る **kiru** (*wear*) _____

3. 食べる **taberu** (*eat*) _____

4. 寝る **neru** (*sleep*) _____

EXERCISE

4·3

The following verbs are all **u** *verbs in the dictionary form. Convert them to the* **masu** *form.*

1. 帰る **kaeru** (*return*) _____

2. 切る **kiru** (*cut*) _____

3. 走る **hashiru** (*run*) _____

4. しゃべる **shaberu** (*chat*) _____

Frequently used verbs

Motion verbs like *to go* and *to come* are very frequently used in daily life. There are many native verbs, and there are also many **suru** verbs—verbs that are created by combining Sino-Japanese vocabulary written in kanji characters and the verb する **suru** (*do*). In addition, many **suru** verbs are made from English. **Suru** verbs conjugate like the verb する **suru**, one of the two major irregular verbs. The following list includes some frequently used Japanese verbs:

buy	買う	**kau**
clean	掃除する	**sōji suru**
come	来る	**kuru**
do	する	**suru**
do laundry	洗濯する	**sentaku suru**
drink	飲む	**nomu**
eat	食べる	**taberu** (**ru** verb)
go	行く	**iku**
make	作る	**tsukuru**
make a copy	コピーする	**kopī suru**
read	読む	**yomu**
return	帰る	**kaeru** (**u** verb)
sleep	寝る	**neru** (**ru** verb)
study	勉強する	**benkyō-suru**
wake up	起きる	**okiru**
write	書く	**kaku**

EXERCISE
4·4

*Write the appropriate Japanese verbs using two forms—the dictionary form and the **masu** form.*

1. *to make* _____

   _____

2. *to read* _____

   _____

3. *to write* _____

   _____

4. *to drink* _____

   _____

5. *to go* _____

   _____

6. *to study* _____

   _____

7. *to come* _____

   _____

EXERCISE
4·5

*The following verbs end in either **-iru** or **-eru**. Do you remember whether they are **ru** verbs or **u** verbs? If not, check the earlier vocabulary list on page 65 or use a dictionary to find their verb class and change them into the **masu** form.*

1. 食べる **taberu** _____

2. 帰る **kaeru** _____

3. 寝る **neru** _____

EXERCISE
4·6

*The following commonly used verbs are not included in the list on page 65. They do not end in -**iru** or -**eru**, so you can be sure that they are **u** verbs. Change them to their **masu** form.*

1. なる **naru** (*become*) _____

2. 売る **uru** (*sell*) _____

3. 取る **toru** (*take*) _____

4. 聞く **kiku** (*listen*) _____

5. 歩く **aruku** (*walk*) _____

6. 貸す **kasu** (*lend*) _____

7. 話す **hanasu** (*speak*) _____

8. 会う **au** (*meet*) _____

9. 洗う **arau** (*wash*) _____

10. 待つ **matsu** (*wait*) _____

11. 持つ **motsu** (*hold*) _____

12. 休む **yasumu** (*rest*) _____

13. 住む **sumu** (*reside, live*) _____

14. 死ぬ **shinu** (*die*) _____

15. 選ぶ **erabu** (*select*) _____

16. 運ぶ **hakobu** (*carry*) _____

EXERCISE
4·7

*The following verbs all end in -**iru** or -**eru**. Compare the two forms of each verb and determine whether it is a **ru** verb or an **u** verb.*

1. 入る **hairu** (*enter*), 入ります **hairimasu** _____

2. 走る **hashiru** (*run*), 走ります **hashirimasu** _____

3. 開ける **akeru** (*open*), 開けます **akemasu** _____

4. 着る **kiru** (*wear*), 着ます **kimasu** _____

5. 閉める **shimeru** (*close*), 閉めます **shimemasu** _____

6. あげる **ageru** (*give*), あげます **agemasu** _____

7. 知る **shiru** (*get to know*), 知ります **shirimasu** _____

8. つける **tsukeru** (*turn on*), つけます **tsukemasu** _____

9. 捨てる **suteru** (*throw away*), 捨てます **sutemasu** _____

10. 覚える **oboeru** (*memorize*), 覚えます **oboemasu** _____

Going to the supermarket

Here you will learn how to express coming and going, how to make a verb negative, and some terms that refer to various places around town. With this knowledge, you will be able to ask someone whether he will go to the supermarket, or reply to such a question.

Showing the destination with に **ni** or へ **e**

To express coming and going, use the verbs 行く **iku**, 来る **kuru**, and 帰る **kaeru** and mark the destination with the particle に **ni** or へ, which is read as **e** rather than **he**. に **ni** has many more functions than the particle へ **e**, and you cannot use them interchangeably all the time. However, for marking where you are going, you can use either one. For example:

> 私はスーパーに行きます。
> **Watashi wa sūpā ni ikimasu.**
> 私はスーパーへ行きます。
> **Watashi wa sūpā e ikimasu.**
> *I'll go to the supermarket.*

The polite non-past negative suffix ません **masen**

ません **masen** is a negative counterpart of ます **masu** and makes the verb negative. For example, 行きません **ikimasen** means *I will not go.*

The negative scope marker は **wa**

The part of a sentence that is negated is usually marked by は **wa**. Using this marker is optional but preferred. It is a little confusing because は **wa** also marks topics (Chapter 2), so you will see は **wa** in both affirmative and negative sentences. For example, compare the two responses to the question あしたはスーパーに行きますか **Ashita wa sūpā ni ikimasu ka** (*Will you go to the supermarket tomorrow?*):

> あしたは行きません。
> **Ashita wa ikimasen.**
> *I won't go there tomorrow (although I might go there the day after tomorrow).*

> スーパーには行きません。
> **Sūpā ni wa ikimasen.**
> *I won't go to the supermarket (although I might go somewhere else tomorrow).*

Places around town

Use the following terms to talk about various places around town:

apartment	アパート	**apāto**
bookstore	本屋	**hon'ya**
cafe	喫茶店	**kissaten**

department store	デパート	**depāto**
home	うち	**uchi**
hospital	病院	**byōin**
karaoke	カラオケ	**karaoke**
library	図書館	**toshokan**
movie theater	映画館	**eigakan**
park	公園	**kōen**
post office	郵便局	**yūbinkyoku**
restaurant	レストラン	**resutoran**
supermarket	スーパー	**sūpā**

Stores: . . . 屋 **ya**

You can refer to some types of stores by using **ya**. For example, bookstores are called either 本屋 **hon'ya** or 書店 **shoten**. The former is more frequently used in conversations than the latter, which is limited in formal situations such as for business. If you go to Japan, you may want to look for the shops and stores in the following list:

(Korean style) barbecue restaurant	焼肉屋	**yakinikuya**
bakery	パン屋	**pan'ya**
bar	飲み屋	**nomiya**
bookstore	本屋	**hon'ya**
fish market	魚屋	**sakanaya**
flower shop	花屋	**hanaya**
Japanese-style bar	居酒屋	**izakaya**
liquor store	酒屋	**sakaya**
meat store	肉屋	**nikuya**
ramen shop	ラーメン屋	**rāmen'ya**
shoe store	靴屋	**kutsuya**
sushi shop	すし屋	**sushiya**
toy store	おもちゃ屋	**omochaya**

EXERCISE
4·8

Match the words in the two columns.

1. デパート **depāto** _____   a. *restaurant*

2. スーパー **sūpā** _____   b. *shoe store*

3. レストラン **resutoran** _____   c. *bakery*

4. うち **uchi** _____   d. *home*

5. 図書館 **toshokan** _____   e. *department store*

6. 本屋 **hon'ya** _____   f. *supermarket*

7. 靴屋 **kutsuya** _____   g. *library*

8. パン屋 **pan'ya** _____   h. *bookstore*

Complete the following short dialogs.

1. A: 今日は図書館に行きますか。

   Kyō wa toshokan ni ikimasu ka.

   B: いいえ , _____。

   Īe, _____.

2. A: 田中さんは今日 _____ か。

   Tanaka-san wa kyō _____ ka.

   B: いいえ, 来ません。

   Īe, kimasen.

3. A: あしたはデパートに行きますか。

   Ashita wa depāto ni ikimasu ka.

   B: はい , _____ 。

   Hai, _____.

4. A: いつうちに_____。

   Itsu uchi ni _____.

   B: あした帰ります。

   Ashita kaerimasu.

Asking "where?" and saying *anywhere*, *somewhere*, and *nowhere*

Here you'll learn how to ask "where?" and "somewhere/anywhere?" and how to reply to such questions with words like *somewhere* or *nowhere*.

Asking "where?"

To ask where someone is going, use the question word どこ **doko**. Just place it where you expect the answer to be and add the particle か **ka** at the end of the sentence. For example:

> 今日はどこに行きますか。
> **Kyō wa doko ni ikimasu ka.**
> *Where are you going today?*

The polite version of どこ **doko** is どちら **dochira**. (See Chapter 2.)

Existential pronouns

To say *somewhere* or *anywhere*, add the particle か **ka** right after the question word どこ **doko**. For example:

> 今日はどこかに行きます。
> **Kyō wa dokoka ni ikimasu.**
> *I will go to somewhere today.*

> 今日はどこかに行きますか。
> **Kyō wa dokoka ni ikimasu ka.**
> *Are you going to anywhere today?*

You can use the same method with other question words, such as だれ **dare** (*who*). The following table provides some examples. The particles が **ga** and を **o** are usually deleted after such existential pronouns.

English	Japanese	Romaji	Examples
someone/anyone	だれか	dareka	だれかと一緒にしますか。 **Dareka to issho ni shimasu ka.** *Will (you) do (it) together with someone?* だれか来ますか。 **Dareka kimasu ka?** *Will someone come?*
somewhere/anywhere	どこか	dokoka	どこかに行きますか。 **Dokoka ni ikimasu ka.** *Will you go somewhere?*
something/anything	何か	nanika	何かと合います。 **Nanika to aimasen.** *(It) will suit with something.* 何か買いますか。 **Nanika kaimasu ka.** *Will you buy something?*

Negative pronouns

If you are going *nowhere*, add も **mo** after どこに **doko ni** and make the verb negative. For example:

> 今日はどこにも行きません。
> **Kyō wa doko ni mo ikimasen.**
> *I will go nowhere today. / I will not go anywhere today.*

You can use the same method with other question words, such as だれ **dare** (*who*). The following table provides some examples. The particle が **ga** and を **o** must be deleted after such existential pronouns.

English	Japanese	Romaji	Examples
no one (not . . . anyone)	だれ . . . も	**dare . . . mo**	だれとも話しません。 **Dare to mo hanashimasen.** *(He) does not talk with anyone.* だれも来ません。 **Dare mo kimasen.** *No one will come.*
nowhere (not . . . anywhere)	どこ . . . も	**doko . . . mo**	どこにも行きません。 **Doko ni mo ikimasen.** *I will not go anywhere.*
nothing (not . . . anything)	何 . . . も	**nani . . . mo**	何とも合いません。 **Nani to mo aimasen.** *(It) does not suit with anything.* 何も買いません。 **Nani mo kaimasen.** *(I) will not buy anything.*

EXERCISE
4·10

Complete the sentences.

1. 今日は _____ 行きますか。

   Kyō wa _____ ikimasu ka.

   Where are you going today?

2. 今日は _____ 行きますか。

   Kyō wa _____ ikimasu ka.

   Will you go to somewhere today?

3. あしたは _____ 。

   Ashita wa _____ .

   I won't go anywhere tomorrow.

EXERCISE
4·11

Translate the following sentences into Japanese.

1. *I will go to the bookstore today.*

   _____

2. *I will not go anywhere tomorrow.*

   _____

3. *Will you go to somewhere tomorrow?*

   _____

4. *Where will you go today?*

   _____

Habitual actions

Habitual actions are actions you do repeatedly, such as daily or weekly. Here you'll learn how to ask someone whether he/she often goes to a certain place. You'll also learn about adverbs related to frequency.

Asking about habitual actions with よく yoku (*often*)

To ask someone whether he/she often goes to a certain place, use the non-past tense of the verb 行く *iku (to go)* and add the frequency adverb よく **yoku**, which means *often*. For example:

田中さんはよくレストランに行きますか。
Tanaka-san wa yoku restoran ni ikimasu ka.
Do you often go to a restaurant, Mr. Tanaka?

Frequency adverbs

The following list shows commonly used frequency adverbs. The adverbs marked with * need to be used with a negative verb, as in the following example:

私はレストランにはあまり行きません。
Watashi wa resutoran ni wa amari ikimasen.
I don't go to restaurants very often.

often	よく	**yoku**
sometimes	ときどき	**tokidoki**
once in a while	たまに	**tamani**
not very often	あまり*	**amari***
rarely . . .	めったに*	**mettani***
never . . .	ぜんぜん*	**zenzen***

EXERCISE
4·12

Translate the following sentences into English.

1. よくレストランに行きます。

   Yoku resutoran ni ikimasu.

   _____

2. ときどきデパートに行きます。

   Tokidoki depāto ni ikimasu.

   _____

3. たまに公園に行きます。

   Tama ni kōen ni ikimasu.

   _____

4. 図書館にはあまり行きません。

Toshokan ni wa amari ikimasen.

_____

5. カラオケにはぜんぜん行きません。

Karaoke ni wa zenzen ikimasen.

_____

EXERCISE
4·13

For each of the following, choose the correct answer from the options in parentheses.

1. よく本屋に（行きます, 行きません）。

   Yoku hon'ya ni (ikimasu, ikimasen).

2. 映画館にはあまり（行きます, 行きません）。

   Eigakan ni wa amari (ikimasu, ikimasen).

3. ときどき居酒屋に（行きます, 行きません）。

   Tokidoki izakaya ni (ikimasu, ikimasen).

Making suggestions

Here you will learn about making suggestions and specifying absolute and approximate times. You will also learn how to express the purpose of going somewhere.

...ませんか **masen ka** and ...ましょう **mashō**

To suggest doing something, use the negative question ending ませんか **masen ka** instead of ます **masu**. If you want to say _Let's do something!_ use ましょう **mashō**. For example:

> レストランに行きませんか。
> **Resutoran ni ikimasen ka.**
> _Why don't we go to a restaurant?_

> レストランに行きましょう。
> **Resutoran ni ikimashō.**
> _Let's go to a restaurant._

If you use ましょう **mashō** in a form of a question, it is understood as a suggestion or offering of help. For example:

> レストランに行きましょうか。
> **Resutoran ni ikimashō ka.**
> _Shall we go to a restaurant?_

> 私が 掃除しましょうか。
> **Watashi ga sōji shimashō ka.**
> _Shall I clean?_

If it includes a question word, it will be used for inviting suggestions:

> どのレストランに行きましょうか。
> **Dono resutoran ni ikimashō ka.**
> *To which restaurant shall we go?*

Specifying an absolute time with に **ni**

To say when, use time expressions such as *tomorrow, next week*, and *on Monday*. After absolute time expressions such as *Monday*, use the particle に **ni**. After relative time expressions such as *tomorrow*, you do not need to use に **ni**. For example:

> 水曜日にすし屋に行きませんか。
> **Suiyōbi ni sushiya ni ikimasen ka.**
> *How about going to a sushi restaurant on Wednesday?*

> 今日すし屋に行きませんか。
> **Kyō sushiya ni ikimasen ka.**
> *How about going to a sushi restaurant today?*

For relative and absolute time expressions, see Chapter 3.

Saying *approximately*

To say *approximately* for quantity, amount, and time expressions, use くらい **kurai** or ぐらい **gurai** after the number phrase. For time expressions, you can also use ごろ **goro**. For example:

> 3時ぐらいに来ます。
> **San-ji gurai ni kimasu.**
> *(He) will come here around 3 o'clock.*

> クッキーを5枚ぐらい食べます。
> **Kukkī o go-mai gurai tabemasu.**
> *(He) eats about five cookies.*

> 5時ごろに来ます。
> **Go-ji goro ni kimasu.**
> *(He) will come here around 5 o'clock.*

Expressing the purpose of going with . . . に行く **ni iku**

Instead of mentioning a destination, you might want to mention the purpose of going. If so, use a verb in the stem form and add the particle に **ni**. The stem form of a verb is usually the form you see before ます **masu** in the **masu** form. Therefore, the stem form is often called *pre-masu* form. For example:

> 映画を見に行きませんか。
> **Eiga o mi ni ikimasen ka.**
> *Why don't we go to see a movie?*

Some nouns can be followed by に**ni** to show the purpose of going. For example, キャンプに行く **kyanpu ni iku** means *to go camping*. The following are some examples of purpose of going, expressed either with a verb stem or a noun:

to go camping	キャンプに行く	**kyanpu ni iku**
to go for a drink	飲みに行く	**nomi ni iku**
to go shopping	買い物に行く	**kaimono ni iku**

to go to buy . . .	...を買いに行く	. . . o kai ni iku
to go to eat . . .	...を食べに行く	. . . o tabe ni iku
to go to see . . .	...を見に行く	. . . o mi ni iku
to visit . . .	...に遊びに行く	. . . ni asobi ni iku

EXERCISE
4·14

Translate the following sentences into English.

1. 今晩映画を見に行きませんか。

   Konban eiga o mi ni ikimasen ka.

   _____

2. キャンプに行きませんか。

   Kyanpu ni ikimasen ka.

   _____

3. 土曜日に買い物に行きませんか。

   Doyōbi ni kaimono ni ikimasen ka.

   _____

4. あした日本語の辞書を買いに行きませんか。

   Ashita Nihongo no jisho o kai ni ikimasen ka.

   _____

5. 来年沖縄に遊びに行きませんか。

   Rainen Okinawa ni asobi ni ikimasen ka.

   _____

6. 来週マイクさんのうちに遊びに行きませんか。

   Raishū Maiku-san no uchi ni asobi ni ikimasen ka.

   _____

7. 何時ごろに行きましょうか。

   Nan-ji goro ni ikimashō ka.

   _____

Translate the following into Japanese.

1. *Will you go to the supermarket today?*

_____

2. *Will you go anywhere tomorrow?*

_____

3. *Why don't we go to Japan next year?*

_____

4. *Do you often go to restaurants?*

_____

5. *I don't go to the library very often.*

_____

6. *Let's go to the park!*

_____

Transportation

Here you'll learn how to specify the form of transportation and the length of time needed to go somewhere. You'll also learn some useful sentence-final particles you can use for getting an agreement for your statement or for emphasizing your statement.

Specifying the form of transportation with で de

To specify how you go somewhere, say the form of the transportation and add the particle で **de**. The particle で **de** is used with many different verbs, but it usually specifies the item or condition used for the action. When the action is going, で **de** specifies the form of transportation. For example, 大阪に車で行きます **Ōsaka ni kuruma de ikimasu** means *(I) will go to Osaka by car*. If you walk somewhere rather than use another form of transportation, use 歩いて **aruite**, which is the **te** form of the 歩く **aruku** *(to walk)*. For example, 歩いて図書館に行きます **Aruite toshokan ni ikimasu** means *I go to the library on foot* or *I walk to the library*. See Chapter 5 for more about the **te** form of verbs.

Words for transportation

Use the following words to refer to different modes of transportation:

airplane	飛行機	**hikōki**
bicycle	自転車	**jitensha**
bus	バス	**basu**
car	車	**kuruma**

ferry	フェリー	**ferī**
shinkansen (bullet train)	新幹線	**shinkansen**
subway	地下鉄	**chikatetsu**
taxi	タクシー	**takushī**
train	電車	**densha**

Counters for hours and minutes

To specify the length of time needed for an activity, use the counters 時間 **jikan** (*hours*) and 分 **fun** (*minutes*) and the verb かかる **kakaru** (*to take, to cost*). For example, 1時間15分かかります **Ichi-jikan jū-go-fun kakarimasu** means *It takes one hour and 15 minutes.* Here we are talking about the length of time needed for an activity rather than the time of day.

Sentence-ending particles ね **ne** and よ **yo**

End a sentence with ね **ne** if you want to get an agreement to your statement. End a sentence with よ **yo** if you want to emphasize your statement. For example:

いい天気ですね。
Ii tenki desu ne.
It's a nice weather, isn't it?

日本語は簡単ですよ。
Nihongo wa kantan desu yo.
Japanese is easy, I tell you!

EXERCISE
4·16

Complete each sentence with the appropriate word or phrase.

1. 私は会社に _____ 行きます。

   Watashi wa kaisha ni _____ ikimasu.

   I drive to my company.

2. 私は大学に _____ 行きます。

   Watashi wa daigaku ni _____ ikimasu.

   I go to my university by a bus and a train.

3. 母はスーパーに _____ 行きます。

   Haha wa sūpā ni _____ ikimasu.

   My mother walks to the supermarket.

4. _____ 帰りませんか。

   _____ **kaerimasen ka.**

   Why don't we go home by taxi?

5. 田中さんは _____ ここに来ました。

   Tanaka-san wa _____ koko ni kimashita.

   Mr. Tanaka came here by bicycle.

EXERCISE
4·17

The following passage was written by Takeshi. Read it carefully and answer the questions that follow.

父は銀行で働いています。銀行にはバスと電車で行きます。バスで15分と電車で30分です。姉は看護師です。病院にはバスで行きます。バスで25分です。私は大学の英語の学生です。大学にはバスと地下鉄で行きます。1時間かかります。

Chichi wa ginkō de hataraite imasu. Ginkō ni wa basu to densha de ikimasu. Basu de jū-go-fun to densha de sanjup-pun desu. Ane wa kangoshi desu. Byōin ni wa basu de ikimasu. Basu de ni-jū-go-fun desu. Watashi wa daigaku no eigo no gakusei desu. Daigaku ni wa basu to chikatetsu de ikimasu. Ichi-jikan kakarimasu.

1. How long does it take for Takeshi's father to commute? _____

2. How about for his sister? _____

3. What modes of transportation does Takeshi use to commute to his school? _____

EXERCISE
4·18

Read the following dialog between Takeshi and George and answer the questions that follow.

TAKESHI   今晩カラオケに行きませんか。

Konban karaoke ni ikimasen ka.

GEORGE   いいですね。行きましょう。

Ii desu ne. Ikimashō.

(いい **ii** means *good*)

TAKESHI   何時ごろ？

Nan-ji goro?

GEORGE   7時は？

Shichi-ji wa?

TAKESHI   いいですよ。孝子さんも雪子さんも誘いましょう。

Ii desu yo. Takako-san mo Yukiko-san mo sasoimashō.

GEORGE   ええ。

Ē.

1. When are they going to karaoke?

   _____

2. Who are going?

   _____

3. What does いいですね **Ii desu ne** in the dialog mean?

   _____

4. What does いいですよ **Ii desu yo** in the dialog mean?

   _____

Talking about activities

This chapter shows you how to express a variety of activities while paying close attention to the time and the aspect of the action using different kinds of adverbs and verb forms. You'll learn how to talk about activities that occur often in your life, activities you've done in the past, and activities you're planning to do. You'll also learn how to express your abilities and how to make requests.

Recurring activities

Here you'll learn how to talk about the activities you do daily, using a variety of verbs for actions.

Words for proportional frequency

Adverbs like *usually* and *always* refer to proportional frequency:

usually	たいてい	**taitei**
always	いつも	**itsumo**

The direct object marker を o

For many actions, you need to specify the item that the action directly affects or applies to. These items are traditionally called *direct objects* in grammar. A direct object can be a thing or a person. In English, we know which noun is the direct object because it immediately follows a verb, without an intervening preposition. By contrast, in Japanese, the word order can be flexible. However, a direct object is clearly marked by the particle を **o**. Read the following sentences and identify the direct object in each:

> 母はよくケーキを作ります。
> **Haha wa yoku kēki o tsukurimasu.**
> *My mother often makes a cake.*

> 誕生日に友達を5人招待します。
> **Tanjōbi ni tomodachi o go-nin shōtai shimasu.**
> *I'll invite five of my friends on my birthday.*

Daily routines

Certain actions are part of the daily routine for almost everyone. For example:

to brush one's teeth	歯を磨く	**ha o migaku**
to get dressed	服を着る	**fuku o kiru**

to go to bed	寝る	neru
to have breakfast	朝ご飯を食べる	asa-gohan o taberu
to have dinner	晩ご飯を食べる	ban-gohan o taberu
to have lunch	昼ご飯を食べる	hiru-gohan o taberu
to take a shower	シャワーを浴びる	shawā o abiru
to wake up	起きる	okiru
to wash one's face	顔を洗う	kao o arau

Specifying the location of activities with で de

To specify the location of an activity, use the particle で **de**. For example:

うちで映画を見ます
Uchi de eiga o mimasu.
I watch a movie at home.

Think of で **de** as marking what is being used for the action. It could be a transportation method, the location of an activity, a tool, or some means. For example:

車で行きます。
Kuruma de ikimasu.
I go there by car.

図書館で勉強します。
Toshokan de benkyō shimasu.
I study at the library.

箸で食べます。
Hashi de tabemasu.
I eat with chopsticks.

日本語で話してください。
Nihon-go de hanashite kudasai.
Please speak in Japanese.

Activities on weekends

What do you do on weekends? Read manga? Watch anime? Practice karate? You can use the following phrases to express what you do on weekends:

to dine	食事をする	shokuji o suru
to go fishing	つりをする	tsuri o suru
to go shopping	買い物をする／買い物に行く	kaimono o suru/kaimono ni iku
to go to a park	公園に行く	kōen ni iku
to have a house party	ホームパーティーをする	hōmupātī o suru
to learn French	フランス語を習う	Furansu-go o narau
to play a game	ゲームをする	gēmu o suru
to play tennis	テニスをする	tenisu o suru
to play the piano	ピアノを弾く	piano o hiku
to play the trumpet	トランペットを吹く	toranpetto o fuku
to read a magazine	雑誌を読む	zasshi o yomu
to read manga (comic books)	漫画を読む	manga o yomu
to read a newspaper	新聞を読む	shinbun o yomu
to run	走る	hashiru
to send an email	メールする	mēru suru
to sing (at karaoke)	（カラオケで）うたう	(karaoke de) utau
to swim	泳ぐ	oyogu

to use a computer	パソコンをする／パソコンを使う	pasokon o suru/ pasokon o tsukau
to walk around in the town	街をブラブラする	machi o burabura suru
to watch a movie	映画を見る	eiga o miru
to watch anime	アニメを見る	anime o miru
to write a letter	手紙を書く	tegami o kaku

The verb *to play*

The English verb *to play* is translated in Japanese differently depending on what is done. For playing a sport or game, use する **suru** (*to do*). For playing a musical instrument, use a verb that applies to the particular instrument—such as 弾く **hiku** for string instrument and keyboard and 吹く **fuku** (*to blow*) for wind instruments. When you're using *to play* as an intransitive verb, as in *Children are playing*, use 遊ぶ **asobu** (*to play*).

EXERCISE
5·1

Translate the following sentences into English.

1. 雑誌を読みます。 **Zasshi o yomimasu**. _____

2. 手紙を書きます。 **Tegami o kakimasu**. _____

3. 映画を見ます。 **Eiga o mimasu**. _____

4. ゲームをします。 **Gēmu o shimasu**. _____

5. ピアノを弾きます。 **Piano o hikimasu**. _____

EXERCISE
5·2

*Complete each of the following sentences with に **ni** or を **o**. For a greater challenge, cover the English translations.*

1. デパート _____ 行きます。

   Depāto _____ ikimasu.

   I will go to a department store.

2. ケーキ _____ 作ります。

   Kēki _____ tsukurimasu.

   I will make a cake.

3. 新聞 _____ 読みます。

   Shinbun _____ yomimasu.

   I will read a newspaper.

   (新聞 **shinbun** means *newspaper*)

4. 映画 (movie) _____ 見ます。

Eiga _____ mimasu.

I will watch a movie.

5. 洋服 (cloth) _____ 買います。

Yōfuku _____ kaimasu.

I will buy clothes.

6. テニス _____ します。

Tenisu _____ shimasu.

I will play tennis.

7. ゲーム _____ します。

Gēmu _____ shimasu.

I will play a game.

8. うち _____ 帰ります。

Uchi _____ kaerimasu.

I will go home.

EXERCISE
5·3

*Complete each of the following sentences with で **de** or に **ni.** For a greater challenge, cover the English translations.*

1. うち _____ 帰ります。

I will go home.

Uchi _____ kaerimasu.

2. うち _____ 寝ます。

Uchi _____ nemasu.

I will sleep at home.

3. タクシー _____ うち _____ 帰ります。

Takushī _____ uchi _____ kaerimasu.

I will go home by taxi.

4. レストラン _____ 行きます。

Resutoran _____ ikimasu.

I will go to a restaurant.

5. レストラン _____ 食べます。

Resutoran _____ tabemasu.

I will eat at a restaurant.

6. 映画館 _____ 映画を見ます。

Eigakan _____ eiga o mimasu.

I will watch a movie at a movie theater.

7. うち _____ パソコン _____ アニメを見ます。

Uchi _____ pasokon _____ anime o mimasu.

I will watch anime at home using a computer.

EXERCISE
5·4

*Complete each of the following sentences with を **o**, で **de**, or に **ni**. For a greater challenge, cover the English translations.*

1. うち _____ ケーキ _____ 食べます。

Uchi _____ kēki _____ tabemasu.

I will eat a cake at home.

2. ケーキ _____ うち _____ 食べます。

Kēki _____ uchi _____ tabemasu.

I will eat a cake at home.

3. 車 _____ ボストン _____ 行きます。

Kuruma _____ Bosuton _____ ikimasu.

I will go to Boston by car.

4. 私はフォークとナイフ _____ 食べます。

Watashi wa fōku to naifu _____ tabemasu.

I eat with a fork and a knife.

5. 母は箸 _____ 食べます。

Haha wa hashi _____ tabemasu.

My mother eats with chopsticks.

6. 兄は空手と剣道 _____ します。

Ani wa karate to kendō _____ shimasu.

My older brother does karate and kendo.

EXERCISE
5·5

Translate the following passage into English.

週末はたいてい午前中に買い物に行きます。 デパートによく行きます。 それから, レスランで
食事をします。 それから, 午後, 映画館で映画を見ます。

**Shūmatsu wa taitei gozenchū ni kaimono ni ikimasu. Depāto ni yoku ikimasu. Sorekara,
resutoran de shokuji o shimasu. Sorekara, gogo, eigakan de eiga o mimasu.**

(それから **sorekara** means *then, in addition*)

_____

_____

_____

_____

EXERCISE
5·6

In Japanese, write what you do on weekends.

_____

_____

_____

_____

Identifying the action performer

In Japanese, the subject noun is marked by the particle が **ga**. The subject noun can be the person who performs the action. If you want to specify the person who accompanies the person for doing the same action, use the particle と **to**.

Specifying the action performer with the subject marker が **ga**

The subject is marked by が **ga**. For example:

> だれがギターを弾きますか。
> **Dare ga gitā o hikimasuka.**
> *Who will play the guitar? / Who plays the guitar?*

> 山田さんが弾きます。
> **Yamada-san ga hikimasu.**
> *Ms. Yamada will play it. / Ms. Yamada plays it.*

The subject noun can also be the topic of the sentence at the same time in many cases. Then, the topic particle は **wa** discussed in Chapter 2 can mark the subject, covering and hiding the particle が **ga**. For example:

> 山田さんはギターを弾きます。
> **Yamada-san wa gitā o hikimasu.**
> *Ms. Yamada will play the guitar. / Ms. Yamada plays the guitar.*

Specifying the accompanying action performer with と **to**

When one does something with someone else, the latter person is marked by the particle と **to**. For example:

> 今日は田中さんが山田さんとうちに来ます。
> **Kyō wa Tanaka-san ga Yamada-san to uchi ni kimasu.**
> *Mr. Tanaka will come to my house with Ms. Yamada today.*

Of course, you can rephrase it like this:

> 今日は田中さんと山田さんがうちに来ます。
> **Kyō wa Tanaka-san to Yamada-san ga uchi ni kimasu.**
> *Mr. Tanaka and Ms. Yamada will come to my house today.*

See Chapter 3 for using the particle と **to** for listing items as in the above sentence.

EXERCISE

5·7

*Complete each of the following sentences with either が **ga** or を **o**. For a greater challenge, cover the English translations.*

1. 田中さんが森さん _____ 招待します。

   Tanaka-san ga Mori-san _____ shōtai-shimasu.

   Mr. Tanaka invites Mr. Mori.

   (招待する **shōtai-suru** means *to invite*)

2. 森さんを田中さん _____ 招待します。

   Mori-san o Tanaka-san _____ shōtai-shimasu.

   Mr. Tanaka invites Mr. Mori.

3. あしたは母 _____ てんぷら _____ 作ります。すしは父 _____ 作ります。

   Ashita wa haha _____ tenpura _____ tsukurimasu. Sushi wa chichi _____ tsukurimasu.

   Tomorrow, my mother will make tempura. My father will make sushi.

4. 田中さんはワイン _____ 買います。

   Tanaka-san wa wain _____ kaimasu.

   Mr. Tanaka will buy a bottle of wine.

*Complete each of the following sentences with と **to** or を **o**. For a greater challenge, cover the English translations.*

1. 父は中国語 _____ 話します。

   Chichi wa Chūgokugo _____ hanashimasu.

   My father speaks Chinese.

2. 母はよく兄 _____ 話します。

   Haha wa yoku ani _____ hanashimasu.

   My mother often speaks with my older brother.

3. 私はときどきうちで姉 _____ うたいます。

   Watashi wa tokidoki uchi de ane _____ utaimasu.

   I sometimes sing with my older sister at home.

4. 私はよくカフェテリアで田中さん _____ 山田さん _____ 見ます。

   Watashi wa yoku kafeteria de Tanaka-san _____ Yamada-san _____ mimasu.

   I often see Mr. Tanaka and Ms. Yamada at the cafeteria.

5. 今日は母 _____ 映画 _____ 見に行きます。

   Kyō wa haha _____ eiga _____ mi ni ikimasu.

   I will go to watch a movie with my mother today.

The following was written by Mika. Read it and answer the questions that follow.

晩ご飯はいつも母が作ります。たいてい姉が手伝います。週末の朝ご飯は私が作ります。よくパンケーキを作ります。日曜日の昼ご飯は家族でレストランで食べます。

Ban-gohan wa itsumo haha ga tsukurimasu. Taitei ane ga tetsudaimasu. Shūmatsu no asa-gohan wa watashi ga tsukurimasu. Yoku pankēki o tsukurimasu. Nichiyōbi no hiru-gohan wa kazoku de resutoran de tabemasu.

(晩ご飯 **ban-gohan** means *dinner;* 手伝う **tetsudau** means *to help;* 朝ご飯 **asa-gohan** means *breakfast;* 昼ご飯 **hiru-gohan** means *lunch;* 家族 で **kazoku de** means *with family*)

1. Who cooks dinner? _____

2. When does Mika cook? _____

3. When do they eat at a restaurant? _____

Talking about the past

To describe some incidents or events in the past, use the past tense of verbs. It is also always effective to connect sentences appropriately, indicating *however*, *then*, *in addition*, or *therefore*.

...ました **mashita** and ませんでした **masendeshita**

To express past actions, replace ます **masu** with ました**mashita** and ません **masen** with ません でした **masendeshita**. For example:

> 漢字を書きました
> **Kanji o kakimashita.**
> *I wrote kanji.*

> 漢字を書きませんでした
> **Kanji o kakimasendeshita.**
> *I did not write kanji.*

The following table summarizes non-past and past forms for both affirmative and negative polite suffixes:

	AFFIRMATIVE	NEGATIVE
Non-past	書きます kakimasu	書きません kakimasen
Past	書きました kakimashita	書きませんでした kakimasendeshita

The colloquial substandard form of the past negative form can be create by changing ない **nai** in the **nai** form with なかったです **nakatta desu**, as in 書かなかったです **kakanakatta desu**. The **nai** form is introduced later in this chapter.

The conjunctions それから **sorekara**, でも **demo**, and ですから **desukara**

When talking about one's actions, it's useful to use a conjunction such as *however*, *then*, *in addition*, or *therefore*. Some useful conjunctions are listed in the following table:

English	Japanese	Romaji	Examples
and then	それから	sorekara	本を読みました。それから,寝ました。 **Hon o yomimashita. Sorekara, nemashita.** *I read a book. Then I went to bed.*
however	でも	demo	森さんは来ました。でも, 谷さんは来ませんでした。 **Mori-san wa kimashita. Demo, Tani-san wa kimasendeshita.** *Mr. Mori came. However, Mr. Tani did not come.*
therefore	ですから	desukara	今日は友達が来ます。ですから, ワインを買います。 **Kyō wa tomodachi ga kimasu. Desukara, wain o kaimasu.** *My friend will come today. So I will buy a bottle of wine.*
in addition	それから	sorekara	週末は新聞を読みます。それから, 映画を見ます。 **Shūmatsu wa shinbun o yomimasu. Sorekara, eiga o mimasu.** *On weekends, I read the newspaper. In addition, I watch a movie.*

For each of the following, choose the appropriate answer from the options in the parentheses. For a greater challenge, cover the English translations.

1. 昨日はテレビを見ました。それから, スパゲッティーを（食べます, 食べました）。

    Kinō wa terebi o mimashita. Sorekara, supagettī o (tabemasu, tabemashita).

    I watched TV yesterday. Then, I ate spaghetti.

2. すしは食べます。でも, さしみは（食べます, 食べません）。

    Sushi wa tabemasu. Demo, sashimi wa (tabemasu, tabemasen).

    I eat sushi. However, I do not eat sashimi.

3. 母は日本人です。ですから, 私は日本語を（話します, 話しません）。

    Haha wa Nihon-jin desu. Desukara, watashi wa Nihon-go o (hanashimasu, hanashimasen).

    My mother is Japanese. So, I speak Japanese.

4. 母は日本人です。でも, 私は日本語を（話します, 話しません）。

    Haha wa Nihon-jin desu. Demo, watashi wa Nihon-go o (hanashimasu, hanashimasen).

    My mother is Japanese. However, I don't speak Japanese.

5. 去年は日本語を勉強しました。でも, 漢字は勉強（しました, しませんでした）。

    Kyonen wa Nihon-go o benkyō-shimashita. Demo, kanji wa benkyō-(shimashita, shimasendeshita).

    I studied Japanese last year. However, I did not study kanji.

Expressing your plans

Here you will learn how to express your intentions and your future plans using the correct verb forms.

...つもりです tsumori desu

To say *I plan to . . .*, use a verb in the plain non-past form and add つもりです **tsumori desu**. You already know the plain non-past affirmative form, which is the dictionary form, introduced in Chapter 4. For example:

> 行くつもりです
> **Iku tsumori desu.**
> *I plan to go.*

The plain non-past negative form always ends in **nai**, so we call it the **nai** form for short. For example:

> 行かないつもりです
> **Ikanai tsumori desu.**
> *I plan not to go.*

Nai form

You make a **nai** form by dropping **ru** or **u** from the dictionary form and adding **nai** or **anai**. The following table lists representative **ru** verbs and **u** verbs as well as the two major irregular verbs in the dictionary form and the **nai** form. To conjugate a verb, find out its verb class (**ru** verb, **u** verb, or irregular verb) and check the ending of the dictionary form, and then follow the pattern of one of the verbs in the following table. Note that when a verb ends in a vowel directly followed by **u**, or in other words, when a verb ends in the hiragana う **u**, its **nai** form is formed by adding わない **wanai** after dropping the final う **u**. For example, the **nai** form of 買う **kau** (*buy*) is 買わない **kawanai**.

Verb Class	Ending of the Dictionary Form		Dictionary Form (Plain non-past affirmative)	Nai Form (Plain non-past negative)
Ru verb	-eる	-eru	かえる kaeru (*change*)	かえない kaenai
	-iる	-iru	きる kiru (*wear*)	きない kinai
U verb	-す	-su	はなす hanasu (*speak*)	はなさない hanasanai
	-く	-ku	かく kaku (*write*)	かかない kakanai
	-ぐ	-gu	およぐ oyogu (*swim*)	およがない oyoganai
	-む	-mu	よむ yomu (*read*)	よまない yomanai
	-ぬ	-nu	しぬ shinu (*die*)	しなない shinanai
	-ぶ	-bu	とぶ tobu (*jump*)	とばない tobanai
	-う	-vowel + u	かう kau (*buy*)	かわない kawanai
	-る	-ru	きる kiru (*cut*)	きらない kiranai
	-つ	-tsu	まつ matsu (*wait*)	またない matanai
Irregular verb			くる kuru (*come*)	こない konai
			する suru (*do*)	しない shinai

EXERCISE
5·11

*Conjugate the following verbs into the **nai** form. The verb class is specified only when it is not predictable based on the ending sound of the verb.*

1. 飲む **nomu** _____

2. うたう **utau** _____

3. 見る **miru** (**ru** verb) _____

4. 走る **hashiru** (**u** verb) _____

5. 作る **tsukuru** _____

6. 来る **kuru** (*irregular*) _____

7. する **suru** (*irregular*) _____

8. 行く **iku** _____

9. 泳ぐ**oyogu** _____

10. 遊ぶ **asobu** _____

11. 待つ **matsu** _____

12. 話す **hanasu** _____

Rephrase the following sentences using つもりです _**tsumori desu**._

1. 来年日本に行きます。

   Rainen Nihon ni ikimasu.

   I will go to Japan next year.

   _____

2. 大学院には行きません。

   Daigakuin ni wa ikimasen.

   I won't to go to graduate school.

   _____

3. 日曜日に掃除と洗濯と買い物をします。

   Nichiyōbi ni sōji to sentaku to kaimono o shimasu.

   I will do cleaning, laundry, and shopping on Sunday.

   _____

4. 今晩は寝ません。

   Konban wa nemasen.

   I won't sleep tonight.

   _____

Telling what you can do: Potential form

To say what you can do, you use a verb in the potential form. For **ru** verbs, drop the final **ru** from the dictionary form and add **rareru**. For example, たべる **taberu** (_to eat_) becomes たべられる **taberareru** (_to be able to eat_). For **u** verbs, drop the final **u** and add **eru**. For example, のむ **nomu** (_to drink_) becomes のめる **nomeru** (_to be able to drink_). The potential form of the verb くる **kuru** (_to come_) is こられる **korareru** (_to be able to come_). To express the potential form of the verb する **suru** (_to do_), use the verb できる **dekiru** (_to be able to do_). To convert a verb to the potential form, look at the following table and follow the pattern of the verb in the same class and with the same ending:

Verb Class	Ending of the Dictionary Form		Dictionary Form (Plain non-past affirmative)	Potential Form *(to be able to do . . .)*
Ru verb	-eる	-eru	かえる **kaeru** *(change)*	かえられる **kaerareru**
	-iる	-iru	きる **kiru** *(wear)*	きられる **kirareru**
U verb	-す	-su	はなす **hanasu** *(speak)*	はなせる **hanaseru**
	-く	-ku	かく **kaku** *(write)*	かける **kakeru**
	-ぐ	-gu	およぐ **oyogu** *(swim)*	およげる **oyogeru**
	-む	-mu	よむ **yomu** *(read)*	よめる **yomeru**
	-ぬ	-nu	しぬ **shinu** *(die)*	しねる **shineru**
	-ぶ	-bu	とぶ **tobu** *(jump)*	とべる **toberu**
	-う	-vowel + **u**	かう **kau** *(buy)*	かえる **kaeru**
	-る	-ru	きる **kiru** *(cut)*	きれる **kireru**
	-つ	-tsu	まつ **matsu** *(wait)*	まてる **materu**
Irregular verb			くる **kuru** *(come)*	こられる **korareru**
			する **suru** *(do)*	できる **dekiru**

A verb in the potential form can conjugate just like another **ru** verb. For example, the potential form of 食べる **taberu** *(to eat)* is 食べられる **taberareru** *(to be able to eat)*. It can be conjugated to 食べられない **taberarenai** *(not to be able to eat)*, and たべられます **taberaremasu** *(to be able to eat,* polite), and 食べられません **taberaremasenn** *(not to be able to eat,* polite). The direct object particle を **o** is usually replaced by the particle が **ga** when the verb is in the potential form. For example:

カタカナで名前を書きます。
Katakana de namae o kakimasu.
I (will) write my name in katakana.

カタカナで名前が書けます。
Katakana de namae ga kakemasu.
I can write my name in katakana.

EXERCISE
5·13

Change the following verb phrases to mean to be able to do, *by using the potential form.*

1. カタカナを書く **katakana o kaku** *(to write katakana)*

_____

2. カタカナで名前を書く **katakana de namae o kaku** *(to write one's name in katakana)*

_____

3. 漢字を読む **kanji o yomu** *(to read kanji)*

_____

4. 日本語を話す **Nihongo o hanasu** (*to speak Japanese*)

_____

5. 日本語で話す **Nihongo de hanasu** (*to speak in Japanese*)

_____

6. てんぷらを作る **tenpura o tsukuru** (*to make tempura*)

_____

7. 車を運転する **kuruma o unten-suru** (*to drive a car*)

_____

Answer the following questions in Japanese based on your situation. For a greater challenge, cover the English translations.

1. 箸で食べられますか。

   Hashi de taberaremasu ka.

   Can you eat with chopsticks?

   _____

2. お酒が飲めますか。

   O-sake ga nomemasu ka.

   Can you drink alcoholic beverages?

   _____

3. カタカナで名前が書けますか。

   Katakana de namae ga kakemasu ka.

   Can you write your name in katakana?

   _____

4. 漢字が読めますか。

   Kanji ga yomemasu ka.

   Can you read kanji characters?

   _____

Making requests

There are many different ways of making a request, but the most common way is to use the verb in the **te** form and add ください **kudasai**.

Te form

The **te** form ends in て **te** or で **de**. For example, the **te** form of かく **kaku** (*write*) is かいて **kaite**, and the **te** form of よむ **yomu** (*read*) is よんで **yonde**. The **te** form of a verb means *do . . . and*. It includes the meaning *and*. So, for example, かいて **kaite** means *write and*. To create the **te** form from a dictionary form, follow these rules:

- For **ru** verbs, drop the final る **ru** and add て **te**.
- For **u** verbs that end in す**su**, change the final syllable to して **shite**.
- For **u** verbs that end in く**ku**, change the final syllable to いて **ite**, and for **u** verbs that end in ぐ **gu**, change the final syllable to いで **ide**.
- For **u** verbs that end in う**u**, る **ru**, or つ **tsu**, change the final syllable to って **tte**.
- For **u** verbs that end in む **mu**, ぬ **nu**, or ぶ **bu**, change the final syllable to んで **nde**.
- The **u** verb いく **iku** is slightly irregular, and its te form is いって **itte**.
- The **te** form of くる **kuru** (*come*) is きて **kite**, and the te form of and する **suru** (*do*) is して **shite**.

These rules are illustrated in the following table:

Verb Class	Ending of the Dictionary Form		Dictionary Form	Te Form
Ru verb	-eる	**-eru**	かえる **kaeru** (*change*)	かえて **kaete**
	-iる	**-iru**	きる **kiru** (*wear*)	きて **kite**
U verb	-す	**-su**	はなす **hanasu** (*speak*)	はなして **hanashite**
	-く	**-ku**	かく **kaku** (*write*)	かいて **kaite**
	-ぐ	**-gu**	およぐ **oyogu** (*swim*)	およいで **oyoide**
	-む	**-mu**	よむ **yomu** (*read*)	よんで **yonde**
	-ぬ	**-nu**	しぬ **shinu** (*die*)	しんで **shinde**
	-ぶ	**-bu**	とぶ **tobu** (*jump*)	とんで **tonde**
	-う	**-vowel + u**	かう **kau** (*buy*)	かって **katte**
	-る	**-ru**	きる **kiru** (*cut*)	きって **kitte**
	-つ	**-tsu**	まつ **matsu** (*wait*)	まって **matte**
Major irregular verb			くる **kuru** (*come*)	きて **kite**
			する **suru** (*do*)	して **shite**
Slightly irregular **u** verb			いく **iku** (*go*)	いって **itte**

You create the negative **te** form of a verb by replacing **nai** in its **nai** form with **nakute** (e.g., たべなくて **tabenakute** *not eat and*) or by adding **de** to its **nai** form (e.g., たべないで **tabenai de** *not eat and*). The **nai** form with **nakute** is used to express a cause-effect relationship, as in *not do . . . and so . . .* The form with **nai de** is used to mean *not do . . . and then . . .*, which actually means *instead of doing . . .* or *without doing . . . .* The negative **te** form you should use depends on the context. See Chapter 8 for more about the **te** form.

Requesting with . . . てください **te kudasai**

ください **kudasai** literally means *please give it to me* when it follows a noun and を **o**. (See Chapter 3 for . . . をください **o kudasai** *please give me . . . .*)

When it follows a verb in the **te** form, it means *Please do . . . .* For example:

東京に行ってください。
Tōkyō ni itte kudasai.
Please go to Tokyo.

When you ask someone not to do something, use the negative **te** form that ends in **nai de**. For example:

東京に行かないでください。
Tōkyō ni ikanai de kudasai.
Please do not go to Tokyo.

EXERCISE
5·15

*Give the **te** form of each of the following verbs.*

1. かく **kaku** (*write*)_____

2. かう **kau** (*buy*) _____

3. いう **iu** (*say*) _____

4. いく **iku** (*go*) _____

5. かつ **katsu** (*win*) _____

6. とぶ **tobu** (*jump*) _____

7. よむ **yomu** (*read*) _____

8. およぐ **oyogu** (*swim*) _____

9. する **suru** (*do*) _____

10. くる **kuru** (*come*) _____

EXERCISE
5·16

What do you say in Japanese if you want to ask someone to do the following?

1. 入る **hairu** (*to enter*)

_____

2. 座る **suwaru** (*to sit down*)

_____

3. 休む **yasumu** (*to rest*)

_____

4. この手紙を読む **kono tegami o yomu** (*to read this letter*)

_____

5. また来る **mata kuru** (*to come again*)

_____

6. タバコをすわない **tabako o suwanai** (*not to smoke*)

_____

7. しゃべらない **shaberanai** (*not to chat*)

_____

8. 静かにする **shizuka ni suru** (*to be quiet*) (See Chapter 7 for the adverb + する **suru** *to do*)

_____

Talking about "now" with . . . ている te iru

You know that the past tense shows what one did and the non-past tense shows what one will do or what one does as a habit. So how do you show an action progressing in the present? To express an action progressing, use a verb in the **te** form and add the verb いる **iru** (*exist*). In this case, いる **iru** is functioning as an auxiliary verb. This construction can also express an action taking place habitually and a state that results from an action.

Progressive state

. . . ている **te iru** can express the state where one is doing something such as eating, drinking, dancing, or studying. It is often used with an adverb like 今 **ima** (*now*). For example:

> 母は今てんぷらを作っています。
> **Haha wa ima tenpura o tsukutte imasu.**
> *My mother is making tempura now.*

Habitual state

. . . ている **te iru** can also express what one does regularly. In this case, you can use an adverb for intervals like 毎日 **mainichi** (*every day*) to clarify the meaning. For example:

> 母は毎日ヨーグルトを食べています。
> **Haha wa mainichi yōguruto o tabete imasu.**
> *My mother is eating yogurt every day.*

Resulting state

. . . ている **te iru** can also express the state that results from a completed action. For example, even if one is not drinking currently, if he is drunk because he drank one hour ago, you can express his current state by using . . . ている **te iru** because the current intoxicated state resulted from the past action of drinking. For example:

> 兄はちょっと変です。お酒を飲んでいますね。
> **Ani wa chotto hen desu. O-sake o nonde imasu ne.**
> *My brother is weird. He is drunk, isn't he?*

Adverbs for intervals

The following adverbs express intervals:

every day	毎日	**mainichi**
every month	毎月	**maitsuki**
every morning	毎朝	**maiasa**
every night	毎晩	**maiban**
every week	毎週	**maishū**
every year	毎年	**maitoshi/mainen**

Adverbs for the aspects of an action

The following adverbs relate to aspects of an action:

continuously	ずっと	**zutto**
yet, still	まだ	**mada**
already	もう	**mō**
already	すでに	**sudeni**

EXERCISE
5·17

What do the following sentences mean in English?

1. 妹は今テレビを見ています。

    Imōto wa ima terebi o mite imasu.

    _____

2. 兄は毎朝 1 時間泳いでいます。

    Ani wa maiasa ichi-jikan oyoide imasu.

    _____

3. 田中さんはまだ来ていません。

    Tanaka-san wa mada kite imasen.

    _____

4. 父は大阪に行っています。

    Chichi wa Ōsaka ni itte imasu.

    _____

5. 姉はもう結婚しています。

    Ane wa mō kekkon shite imasu.

    _____

    (結婚する **kekkon-suru** means *to get married*)

6. 弟は朝からずっとゲームをしています。

    Otōto wa asa kara zutto gēmu o shite imasu.

    _____

Describe in Japanese what your family members are doing now.

_____

_____

_____

Ken and Takako are talking. Read their dialog and answer the questions that follow.

KEN 貴子さんは週末はたいてい何をしていますか。

Takako-san wa shūmatsu wa taitei nani o shite imasu ka.

TAKAKO 週末は走ります。それから, テニスをします。それから, 空手もします。

Shūmatsu wa hashirimasu. Sorekara, tenisu o shimasu. Sorekara, karate mo shimasu.

KEN へえ, すごいですね。僕はスポーツはぜんぜんしませんよ。

Hē, sugoi desu ne. Boku wa supōtsu wa zenzen shimasen yo.

(すごい **sugoi** means *Great!*)

TAKAKO そうですか。

Sō desu ka.

KEN はい。僕は週末はいつも料理をしています。

Hai. Boku wa shūmatsu wa itsumo ryōri o shite imasu.

TAKAKO え?料理を?

E? Ryōri o?

KEN はい。フランス料理もスペイン料理もできます。

Hai. Furansu-ryōri mo Supein-ryōri mo dekimasu.

TAKAKO すごい!

Sugoi!

KEN 今週の週末遊びに来ませんか。何か料理します。

Konshū no shūmatsu asobi ni kimasen ka. Nanika ryōri shimasu.

TAKAKO 本当に?

Hontō ni?

KEN   ええ。

          Ē.

TAKAKO   うれしい!ありがとうございます。じゃあ, 私はワインを持って行きます。

          Ureshii! Arigatō gozaimasu. Jā, watashi wa wain o motte ikimasu.

KEN   いいえ, 何も持って来ないでください。

          Īe, nani mo motte konai de kudasai.

          (持って行く/ 持って来る **motte iku/motte kuru** means *to bring something*)

1. What does Takako do on weekends?

   _____

2. What does Ken do on weekends?

   _____

3. What is Takako's plan for this weekend?

   _____

Talking about people and things and their locations

·6·

This chapter introduces existential verbs and shows how they are frequently used to express the existence of things and people or their locations. It also introduces a lot of words for animals, plants, and home-related terms such as rooms in a house and household items. You'll also learn how to give directions, how to express human relationships, and how to talk about events and incidents using existential verbs.

Existential verbs ある **aru**, いる **iru**, and いらっしゃる **irassharu**

The existential verbs ある **aru**, いる **iru**, and いらっしゃる **irassharu** are used to express the existence of something or someone as well as where he/she/it is. The person or thing that exists is the subject noun, and it is marked by the particle が **ga** unless it functions as a topic at the same time. On the other hand, the location where something or someone exists is marked by the particle に **ni**. ある **aru** (*to exist*) is used for inanimate items. ある **aru** is a slightly irregular **u** verb: its **nai** form is ない **nai**. いる **iru** (*to exist*) is used for animate items such as people and animals. It is a **ru** verb. いらっしゃる **irassharu** (*to exist*) is the polite version of いる **iru** and is used for people to whom the speaker wants to show respect, such as his teacher and boss. いらっしゃる **irassharu** is also a slightly irregular **u** verb: its stem form is いらっしゃり **irasshari** as you would correctly predict, but its masu-form is いらっしゃいます **irasshaimasu**. The major forms of these three existential verbs are summarized in the following table. The symbol * marks the slightly irregular forms.

Dictionary Form	ある aru	いる iru	いらっしゃる irassharu
Verb Class	u verb	ru verb	u verb
Nai Form	*ない nai	いない inai	いらっしゃらない irassharanai
Stem Form	あり ari	い i	いらっしゃり irasshari
Masu Form	あります arimasu	います imasu	*いらっしゃいます irasshaimasu
Te Form	あって atte	いて ite	いらっしゃって irasshatte

Pronouns for locations

The following demonstrative pronouns for locations are parallel to demonstrative pronouns for things discussed in Chapter 2:

here	ここ	koko
there near you	そこ	soko
over there	あそこ	asoko

Animals

動物 **dōbutsu** means *animal*. The following are words for some animals you may see in your neighborhood or at a zoo:

dog	犬	inu
bear	熊	kuma
bird	鳥	tori
cat	猫	neko
cow	牛	ushi
deer	鹿	shika
elephant	象	zō
lion	ライオソ	raion
goldfish	金魚	kingyo
horse	馬	uma
pig	豚	buta
rabbit	兎	usagi
squirrel	りす	risu

Plants

植物 **shokubutsu** means *plant*. The following are words for some plants you may see in your backyard or at a park:

bamboo	竹	take
carnation	カーネーション	kānēshon
cherry blossoms	桜の花	sakura no hana
cherry trees	桜の木	sakura no ki
chrysanthemum	菊	kiku
flower	花	hana
pine tree	松の木	matsu no ki
plum tree	梅の木	ume no ki
rose	ばら	bara
sunflower	ひまわり	himawari
tree	木	ki
tulip	チューリップ	chūrippu

. . . に(は) . . . があります／います . . . ni (wa) . . . ga arimasu/imasu

If you want to express the existence of something, such as say with surprise, "Look! There is a cherry tree over there!" or simply telling what is in some place, as in "There is a cherry tree in my yard," use an existential verb and mark the item with the subject particle が **ga**. For example:

あそこに桜の木があります。
Asoko ni sakura no ki ga arimasu.
There is a cherry tree over there.

うちの裏庭には桜の木があります。
Uchi no uraniwa ni wa sakura no ki ga arimasu.
There is a cherry tree in my backyard.

The same applies to the verbs いる **iru** and いらっしゃる **irassharu**. For example:

あ！あそこに兎がいますよ。
A! Asoko ni usagi ga imasu yo.
Oh! There is a rabbit over there!

あそこに田中先生がいらっしゃいますね。
Asoko ni Tanaka sensei ga irasshaimasu ne.
Professor Tanaka is over there, isn't she?

...は...にあります/います ...wa ...ni arimasu/imasu

If you want to express the location of something, use an existential verb and mark the item with the topic particle は **wa**. For example:

山田さんの店は桜通りにあります。
Yamada-san no mise wa Sakura-dōri ni arimasu.
Ms. Yamada's store is located on Sakura Street.

The same applies to いる **iru** and いらっしゃる **irassharu**. For example:

山田さんはあそこにいます。
Yamada-san wa asoko ni imasu.
Ms. Yamada is over there.

山田先生はあそこにいらっしゃいます。
Yamada-sensei wa asako ni irasshaimasu.
Professor Yamada is over there.

So, if you want to ask the location of someone or something, say it and add は **wa**, and then say とこに **doko ni** and one of the existential verbs. For example:

田中さんはどこにいますか。
Tanaka-san wa doko ni imasu ka.
Where is Mr. Tanaka?

EXERCISE

6·1

Mach the items in the two columns.

1. 犬 **inu** _____   a. *horse*

2. 猫 **neko** _____   b. *rabbit*

3. 馬 **uma** _____   c. *goldfish*

4. 金魚 **kingyo** _____ d. *dog*

5. 兎 **usagi** _____   e. *cat*

EXERCISE 6·2

Mach the items in the two columns.

1. チューリップ **chūrippu** _____   a. *sunflower*

2. ばら **bara** _____   b. *tulip*

3. 桜の木 **sakura no ki** _____   c. *rose*

4. ひまわり **himawari** _____   d. *cherry tree*

5. カーネーション **kānēshon** _____   e. *chrysanthemum*

6. 菊 **kiku** _____   f. *carnation*

EXERCISE 6·3

For each of the following, choose the appropriate answer from the items in the parentheses.

1. あそこにレストランが（あります, います, いらっしゃいます）。

   Asoko ni resutoran ga (arimasu, imasu, irasshaimasu).

2. あそこに兎が（あります, います, いらっしゃいます）。

   Asoko ni usagi ba (arimasu, imasu, irasshaimasu).

3. あそこに女の子が（あります, います, いらっしゃいます）。

   Asoko ni onna no ko ga (arimasu, imasu, irasshaimasu).

4. あそこに先生が（あります, います, いらっしゃいます）。

   Asoko ni sensei ga (arimasu, imasu, irasshaimasu).

5. あそこに桜の木が（あります, います, いらっしゃいます）。

   Asoko ni sakura no ki ga (arimasu, imasu, irasshaimasu).

EXERCISE 6·4

What would you say in Japanese in the following situations?

1. You want to find out where Mt. Fuji is located.

   _____

2. You want to say that there are dogs in Ms. Yamada's house.

   _____

3. You want to know where Mr. Tanaka is.

   _____

4. Someone is wondering where Mr. Tanaka is, and you want to say that he is at the library.

   _____

5. You've just noticed Mary in the distance, and you want to tell your friend who is sitting next to you about it.

   _____

In a house

To express what you have or what you don't have in your house, start with うちには **uchi ni wa** and then the noun marked with the subject particle が **ga**, and end your sentence with an existential verb. You can also include a number phrase, as discussed in Chapter 3. For example:

> うちには寝室が3つあります。
> **Uchi ni wa shinshitsu ga mittsu arimasu.**
> _Our house has three bedrooms._

> うちには車庫がありません。
> **Uchi ni wa shako ga arimasen.**
> _We don't have a garage in our house._

> うちには冷蔵庫が2台あります。
> **Uchi ni wa reizōko ga ni-dai arimasu.**
> _We have two refrigerators in our house._

Rooms and areas in a house

In almost all Japanese houses, people take off their shoes at the entryway. They might have Japanese-style rooms and/or Western-style rooms. The Japanese style is to have the toilet in a separate room from the bathing room. The following terms are used for rooms and areas in a house:

attic*	屋根裏部屋	**yaneurabeya**
basement*	地下室	**chikashitsu**
bathroom (for bathing)	風呂場	**furoba**
bathroom (toilet room)	お手洗い／トイレ	**otearai / toire**
bedroom	寝室	**shinshitsu**
dining room	ダイニング／食堂	**dainingu / shokudō**
entryway	玄関	**genkan**
garage	車庫	**shako**
Japanese-style room	和室	**washitsu**
kitchen	キッチン／台所	**kitchin / daidokoro**
living room	リビング／居間	**ribingu / ima**
office	書斎	**shosai**
closet for futon and other items	押入れ	**oshiire**
room	部屋	**heya**
sunroom*	サンルーム	**sanrūmu**
Western-style room	洋室	**yōshitsu**
yard/garden	庭	**niwa**

---

*Japanese houses rarely have a basement, an attic, or a sunroom.

Household items

Do you have the following items in your home or apartment?

TV	テレビ	**terebi**
car	車	**kuruma**
computer, PC	パソコン	**pasokon**
dryer	乾燥機	**kansōki**
microwave	電子レンジ	**denshi renji**
printer	プリンター	**purintā**
refrigerator	冷蔵庫	**reizōko**
sofa	ソファー	**sofā**
table	テーブル	**tēburu**
washer	洗濯機	**sentakuki**

Things in a bedroom

The following terms are used for things in a bedroom:

bed	ベッド	**beddo**
bookshelf	本箱／本棚	**honbako/hondana**
chair	椅子	**isu**
chest of drawers	たんす	**tansu**
computer, PC	パソコン	**pasokon**
desk	机	**tsukue**
doll	人形	**ningyō**
trash can	ごみ箱	**gomibako**
vase	花瓶	**kabin**

EXERCISE 6·5

Write the following words in Japanese.

1. *TV* _____

2. *refrigerator* _____

3. *bed* _____

4. *chair* _____

5. *desk* _____

EXERCISE 6·6

Answer the following questions for your own situation.

1. (あなたの)うちにはテレビが何台ありますか。

   (Anata no) uchi ni wa terebi ga nan-dai arimasu ka.

2. 冷蔵庫は何台ありますか。

Reizōko wa nan-dai arimasu ka.

_____

3. パソコンは何台ありますか。

Pasokon wa nan-dai arimasu ka.

_____

Translate the following sentences into Japanese.

1. _There are three TVs at Mike's house._

_____

2. _There is no yard in Ms. Mori's house._

_____

3. _There is a basement room in Mary's house._

_____

4. _There is no washer and dryer in George's apartment._

_____

Read the following passage and answer the questions that follow.

私の部屋には机が一つとベッドが一つと椅子が3つあります。それから本箱が一つとテーブルが1つあります。雑誌が5冊あります。それから漫画とゲームソフトがたくさんあります。

Watashi no heya ni wa tsukue ga hito-tsu to beddo ga hito-tsu to isu ga mit-tsu arimasu. Sorekara honbako ga hito-tsu to tēburu ga hito-tsu arimasu. Zasshi ga go-satsu arimasu. Sorekara manga to gēmusofuto ga takusan arimasu.

1. How many chairs are there?

_____

2. How many tables are there?

_____

3. How many magazines are there?

_____

Describe what you have in your room.

_____

_____

_____

_____

Expressing where things are

You can describe where things are relative to other things by using relative location words or compass directions.

Relative location words

To describe the location of things and buildings, use relative location words, such as 上 **ue** (*top/ upper area*) or 近く **chikaku** (*nearby area*), along with the reference item. For example:

雑誌はテーブルの上にあります。
Zasshi wa tēburu no ue ni arimasu.
The magazines are on the table.

銀行は駅の近くにあります。
Ginkō wa eki no chikaku ni arimasu.
The bank is near the train station.

The following table lists a number of relative location words and provides examples of their use:

English	Japanese	Example Sentences
top/upper area	上 **ue**	辞書は机の上にあります。 **Jisho wa tsukue no ue ni arimasu.** *The dictionary is on the desk.*
bottom/lower area	下 **shita**	猫はテーブルの下にいます。 **Neko wa tēburu no shita ni imasu.** *The cat is under the table.*
inside	中 **naka**	携帯はかばんの中にあります。 **Keitai wa kaban no naka ni arimasu.** *The cell phone is in the bag.*
right	右 **migi**	かばんは机の右にあります。 **Kaban wa tsukue no migi ni arimasu.** *The bag is on the right of the desk.*
left	左 **hidari**	かばんは机の左にあります。 **Kaban wa tsukue no hidari ni arimasu.** *The bag is on the left of the desk.*

English	Japanese	Example Sentences
front	前 **mae**	田中さんは山田さんの前にいます。 **Tanaka-san wa Yamada-san no mae ni imasu.** *Mr. Tanaka is in front of Ms. Yamada.*
rear, back	後ろ **ushiro**	高橋さんは山田さんの後ろにいます。 **Takahashi-san wa Yamada-san no ushiro ni imasu.** *Mr. Takahashi is behind Ms. Yamada.*
between	間 **aida**	郵便局は病院と銀行の間にあります。 **Yūbinkyoku wa byōin to ginkō no aida ni arimasu.** *The post office is between the hospital and the bank.*
vicinity, near	近く **chikaku**, そば **soba**	本屋は大学の近くにあります。 **Hon'ya wa daigaku no chikaku ni arimasu.** 本屋は大学のそばにあります。 **Hon'ya wa daigaku no soba ni arimasu.** *The bookstore is near the university.*
side	横 **yoko**	本箱は机の横にあります。 **Honbako wa tsukue no yoko ni arimasu.** *The bookcase is on the side of the desk.*
next to	隣 **tonari**	マイクさんは私の隣にいます。 **Maiku-san wa watashi no tonari ni imasu.** *Mike is next to me.* 銀行はスーパーの隣にあります。 **Ginkō wa sūpā no tonari ni arimasu.** *The bank is next to the supermarket.*

Compass directions

The following terms are used for compass directions:

north	北	**kita**
south	南	**minami**
east	東	**higashi**
west	西	**nishi**

EXERCISE
6·10

Translate the following sentences about someone's room into Japanese.

1. *The bookcase is on the side of the desk.*

   _____

2. *The desk is in front of the window.*

   _____

(窓 **mado** means *window*)

3. The dictionary is in the desk drawer.

4. The sofa is between the desk and the bed.

EXERCISE
6·11

Translate the following sentences about a town into Japanese.

1. The post office is on the south of the university.

2. The restaurant is between the hospital and the bookstore.

3. The bank is next to the city hall.

4. My apartment is near the elementary school.

EXERCISE
6·12

Read the following passage written by Keiko and answer the questions that follow.

駅は町の中心にあります。郵便局は小学校の北にあります。消防署は小学校の前にあります。病院は三番通りにあります。図書館も三番通りにあります。銀行は桜通りにあります。スーパーは病院の隣にあります。私のうちからスーパーまで自転車で5分です。

Eki wa machi no chūshin ni arimasu. Yūbinkyoku wa shōgakkō no kita ni arimasu. Shōbōsho wa shōgakkō no mae ni arimasu. Byōin wa sanban-dōri ni arimasu. Toshokan mo sanban-dōri ni arimasu. Ginkō wa Sakura-dōri ni arimasu. Sūpā wa byōin no tonari ni arimasu. Watashi no uchi kara sūpā made jitensha de go-fun desu.

(駅 **eki** means *train station*; 町 **machi** means *town*; 中心 **chūshin** means *center*; . . . 通り **dōri** means . . . *Street*)

1. Where is the train station?

2. Where is the bank located?

3. How long does it take to go from Keiko's house to the supermarket?

Giving directions

To give directions in Japanese, you must know some words for landmarks such as 交差点 **kōsaten** (*intersection*) and 橋 **hashi** (*bridge*) along with the ordinal counter creater . . .目 **me** (. . .*th*). You must also know some verbs of movement such as 曲がる **magaru** (*to make a turn*) and 渡る **wataru** (*to cross*). It is helpful to connect sentences in your directions with conjunctions such as それから **sorekara** and そうすると **sōsuruto**; both of them mean *then* with different usage.

Useful landmarks for giving directions

The following are some words for landmarks you may need in giving directions:

bridge	橋	**hashi**
bus stop	バス停	**basu-tē**
corner	角	**kado**
end of the street	つきあたり	**tsukiatari**
intersection	交差点	**kōsaten**
koban (police box)	交番	**kōban**
railway crossing	踏み切り	**fumikiri**
road	道	**michi**
stop sign	一時停止	**ichji-tēshi**
straight	まっすぐ	**massugu**
street	通り	**tōri**
. . . Street	. . .通り	**. . . dōri**
traffic light	信号	**shingō**
train station	駅	**eki**

Actions needed for giving directions

The following are some verbs for movement you may need in giving directions:

to cross	渡る	**wataru**
to go	行く	**iku**
to make a turn	曲がる	**magaru**
to pass	過ぎる	**sugiru**
to walk	歩く	**aruku**

Marking the area covered by movement with を o

The particle を **o** can be used with a verb that expresses movement such as going, crossing, turning, or passing. For example:

> この道をまっすぐ行ってください。
> **Kono michi o massugu itte kudasai.**
> *Please go straight on this street.*

Marking the direction with に ni

The particle に **ni** can mark the direction for movement, such as *to the right*, *to the left*, *to the north*, and *to the south*. For example:

> 右に曲がってください。
> **Migi ni magatte kudasai.**
> *Please make a right turn.*

The conjunction そうすると **sōsuruto** (*then*)

そうすると **sōsuruto** can show "automatic results," or something that always happens when used in the non-past tense. For example:

> この道をまっすぐ行ってください。そうすると, 右に銀行があります。
> **Kono michi o massugu itte kudasai. Sōsuruto, migi ni ginkō ga arimasu.**
> *Please go straight on this road. Then you'll see a bank on your right.*

The ordinal counter creator . . . 目 **me**

To say *first*, *second*, *third*, etc., you can add 目 **me** to any numeral-counter combination. For example:

> 3冊目の本
> **san-satsu-me no hon**
> *the third book*

> 2つ目の交差点
> **futa-tsu-me no kōsaten**
> *the second intersection*

EXERCISE

6·13

Translate the following sentences into Japanese.

1. *Please go straight on this street.*

   _____

2. *Please make a left turn at that intersection.*

   _____

3. *Please pass the bus stop.*

   _____

4. *Please cross that bridge.*

   _____

5. *Please make a right turn at the third corner.*

   _____

EXERCISE
6·14

*Following are directions to Michiko's house. Complete them with the correct particles. Note that the demonstrative adjective その **sono** can be used for things that the people conversing cannot see but that the speaker knows about and mentions in the discourse.*

この道をまっすぐ行ってください。それから三つ目 _____ 交差点を右 _____ 曲がってください。そうすると踏み切りがあります。その踏み切り _____ 渡ってください。それから5分ぐらい歩いてください。そうすると右にパン屋 _____ あります。私のアパートはそのパン屋の隣にあります。

Kono michi o massugu itte kudasai. Sorekara mit-tsu me _____ kōsaten o migi _____ magatte kudasai. Sōsuruto fumikiri ga arimasu. Sono fumikiri _____ watatte kudasai. Sorekara go-fun gurai aruite kudasai. Sōsuruto migi ni pan'ya _____ arimasu. Watashi no apāto wa sono pan'ya no tonari ni arimasu.

Expressing human relationships

You can use いる **iru** to express what human relationships you have. For example:

私は日本人の友達が3人います。
Watashi wa Nihon-jin no tomodachi ga san-nin imasu.
I have three Japanese friends.

The following words describe human relationships:

friend	友達	**tomodachi**
acquaintance	知人	**chijin**
aunt	おば／おばさん	**oba/obasan**
best friend	親友	**shin'yū**
boyfriend	彼	**kare**
cousin	いとこ	**itoko**
fiancé	婚約者／フィアンセ	**kon'yakusha/fianse**
girlfriend	彼女	**kanojo**
grandfather	祖父／おじいさん	**sofu/ojīsan**
grandmother	祖母／おばあさん	**sobo/obāsan**
relatives	親戚	**shinseki**
siblings	兄弟	**kyōdai**
uncle	おじ／おじさん	**oji/ojisan**

Translate the following sentences into English.

1. 私は妹が二人います。

   Watashi wa imōto ga futari imasu.

   _____

2. 私は妹が二人と弟が一人います。

   Watashi wa imōto ga futari to otōto ga hitori imasu.

   _____

3. 山田さんは兄弟がいますか。

   Yamada-san wa kyōdai ga imasu ka.

   _____

4. 私は兄弟がいません。

   Watashi wa kyōdai ga imasen.

   _____

5. 兄は婚約者がいます。

   Ani wa kon'yakusha ga imasu.

   _____

6. チェンさんはいとこが 30 人います。

   Chen-san wa itoko ga san-jū-nin imasu.

   _____

Read the following dialog between Keiko and Mary and answer the questions that follow.

KEIKO　メアリーさんは兄弟がいますか。

　　　　Mearī-san wa kyōdai ga imasu ka.

MARY　いいえ, いません。

　　　　Īe, imasen.

KEIKO　ああ。じゃあ, 一人っ子ですか。

　　　　Ā. Jā, hitorikko desu ka.

MARY　はい。恵子さんは?

　　　　Hai. Keiko-san wa?

KEIKO	私は姉が二人と妹が一人います。
	Watashi wa ane ga futari to imōto ga hitori imasu.
MARY	え。本当ですか。
	E. Hontō desu ka.
KEIKO	はい。
	Hai.
MARY	いいですね。
	Ii desu ne.
KEIKO	メアリーさんはいとこはいますか。
	Mearī-san wa itoko wa imasu ka.
MARY	いとこは一人います。
	Itoko wa hitori imasu.

1. How many siblings does Mary have?

   _____

2. What do you think the underlined part of the dialog means?

   _____

3. How many cousins does Mary have?

   _____

4. How many siblings does Keiko have?

   _____

Expressing events and incidents

By using the verb ある **aru**, you can express events and incidents. Note that the locations of events and incidents are marked by で **de** rather than by に **ni** even though an existential verb is used. For example:

> 今日は大阪で面接があります。
> **Kyō wa Ōsaka de mensetsu ga arimasu in.**
> *I have an interview today in Osaka.*

> 今朝仙台で地震がありました。
> **Kesa Sendai de jishin ga arimashita.**
> *There was an earthquake in Sendai this morning.*

Some natural disasters are expressed using verbs such as 来る **kuru** (*come*), なる **naru** (*become*), おきる **okiru** (*occur/take place*), and 発生する **hassei suru** (*occur/take place*).

Words for scheduled events

The following terms are used to describe commonly occurring events:

exam	試験	**shiken**
class	授業	**jugyō**
conference	会議	**kaigi**
date	デート	**dēto**
interview	面接	**mensetsu**
part-time job	バイト	**baito**
party	パーティー	**pātī**
work/job	仕事	**shigoto**

Words for accidents, incidents, and disasters

The following terms are used to describe unscheduled events, such as accidents, incidents, and disasters:

fire	火事, 火災	**kaji, kasai**
accident	事故	**jiko**
disaster	災害	**saigai**
earthquake	地震	**jishin**
explosion	爆発	**bakuhatsu**
flooding	洪水	**kōzui**
mountain fire	山火事	**yama-kaji**
storm	嵐	**arashi**
tornado	竜巻	**tatsumaki**
tsunami	津波	**tsunami**

The conjunction それで **sorede** (*as a result*)

それで **sorede** shows an *expected result* or *resulting decision*. Do not use it to express commands, requests, suggestions, invitations, conjectures, or the speaker's volition.

大阪で会議がありました。それで大阪に一週間いました。
Ōsaka de kaigi ga arimashita. Sorede Ōsaka ni is-shūkan imashita.
There was a conference in Osaka. So I was in Osaka for one week.

仙台で大きい地震がありました。それで津波が来ました。
Sendai de ōkii jishin ga arimashita. Sorede tsunami ga kimashita.
There was a big earthquake in Sendai. As a result, a tsunami hit there.

**EXERCISE
6·17**

Translate the following sentences into English.

1. 今日は授業が３つあります。ですから仕事には行きません。

    Kyō wa jugyō ga mittsu arimasu. Desukara shigoto ni wa ikimasen.

    _____

2. 今日は仕事がありません。ですからいっしょに買い物に行きませんか。

    Kyō wa shigoto ga arimasen. Desukara isshoni kaimono ni ikimasen ka.

    _____

3. 明日は面接と試験があります。それで今日はどこにも行けません。

Ashita wa mensetsu to shiken ga arimasu. Sorede kyō wa doko ni mo ikemasen.

_____

_____

Read the following paragraph written by Seiji and answer the questions that follow.

月曜日と水曜日と金曜日は日本語のクラスがあります。9時から10時までです。金曜日の晩は日本のレストランでバイトがあります。5時から10時までです。

Getsuyōbi to Suiyōbi to Kinyōbi wa Nihon-go no kurasu ga arimasu. Ku-ji kara jū-ji made desu. Kinyōbi no ban wa Nihon no resutoran de baito ga airmasu. Go-ji kara jū-ji made desu.

(. . . から **kara** . . . まで **made** means _from . . . to . . ._)

1. Which days does Seiji have classes?

_____

2. Which days does he have to work?

_____

3. From what time to what time does he have to work?

_____

_____

List your weekly schedule in Japanese.

_____

_____

_____

_____

Read the following passage and answer the questions that follow.

2011 年3月11日に日本の東北地方の近くの太平洋沖でマグニチュード9の地震がおきました。それ
で東北地方に大きい津波が来ました。火災も原子力発電所の事故もおきました。

**Ni-sen-jū-ichi-nen san-gatsu jū-ichi-nichi ni Nihon no Tōhoku Chihō no chikaku no Taiheiyō
oki de magunichūdo kyū no jishin ga okimashita. Sorede Tōhoku Chihō ni ōkii tsunami ga
kimashita. Kasai mo genshiryoku hatsudensho no jiko mo okimashita.**

(東北地方 **Tōhoku Chihō** means *Tohoku Region,* the northeastern portion of Honshu in Japan;
太平洋 **Taiheiyō** means *Pacific Ocean;* 沖 **oki** means *open sea;* 原子力発電所 **genshiryoku
hatsudensho** means *nuclear power plant*)

1. When did the earthquake occur?

   _____

2. Where did it occur?

   _____

3. What was the result?

   _____

Describing things

This chapter shows you how to describe people and things using adjectives in a variety of contexts. You'll learn how to describe buildings, rooms, character traits, appearances, places, seasons, meals, flavors, and clothing. You'll also learn about adverbs derived from adjectives and comparisons.

Adjective types

Every Japanese adjective ends in い **i** or な **na** when placed before a noun. The adjectives that end in い **i** are called *i adjectives* and those that end in な **na** are called *na adjectives*. For example, 高い本 **takai hon** and 高価な本 **kōka na hon** both mean *an expensive book*, but 高い is an i adjective and 高価な is a **na** adjective. The part of the adjective without the ending い **i** or な **na** (e.g., 高 **taka** and 高価 **kōka**) is called the *stem*. 大きい **ōkii** and 小さい **chīsai** are slightly exceptional. They are i adjectives, but when used before a noun, they have additional forms: 大きな **ōki na** and 小さな **chīsa na**.

Adjectives can also be used to end a sentence. For i adjectives, keep the い **i** and add です **desu**. For **na** adjectives, add です **desu** right after the stem, without な **na** before です **desu**.

EXERCISE
7·1

In each of the following sentences, drop the noun and make the appropriate changes to the adjective, as shown in the examples.

EXAMPLE   大きい犬です。 **Ōkii inu desu.** (*It's a big dog.*)

           <u>大きいです。 **Ōkii desu.** (*It's big.*)</u>

           静かな犬です。   **Shizuka na inu desu.** (*It's a quiet dog.*)

           <u>静かです。   **Shizuka desu.** (*It's quiet.*)</u>

1. 新しい車です。**Atarashii kuruma desu.** (*It's a new car.*)

_____

2. きれいな人です。**Kirei na hito desu.** (*She is a pretty person.*)

_____

3. にぎやかなところです。 **Nigiyaka na tokoro desu.** (*It's a crowded and lively place.*)

_____

4. 難しい漢字です。 **Muzukashii kanji desu.** (*It's a difficult kanji character.*)

_____

5. おいしいケーキです。 **Oishii kēki desu.** (*It's a delicious cake.*)

_____

Describing buildings and rooms

Here you will learn how to use adjectives to describe buildings and rooms, and you'll learn what to say when you enter someone's house or apartment.

Adjectives in the non-past forms

See how adjectives pattern in a non-past neutral-polite context in the following table:

	I Adjectives (e.g., 高い **takai** *expensive*)	Na Adjectives (e.g., 高価な **kōka na** *expensive*)
Affirmative	Stem + いです Stem + **i desu** 高いです **takai desu** *is expensive*	Stem + です Stem + **desu** 高価です **kōka desu** *is expensive*
Negative	Stem + くありません Stem + **ku arimasen** *or* Stem + くないです Stem + **ku nai desu** 高くありません **takaku arimasen** 高くないです **takaku nai desu** *isn't expensive*	Stem + じゃありません Stem + **ja arimasen**★ *or* Stem + じゃないです Stem + **ja nai desu**★ 高価じゃありません **kōka ja arimasen** 高価じゃないです **kōka ja nai desu** *isn't expensive*

The negative form of いいです **ii desu** (*is good*) is よくありません **yoku arimasen** or よくないです **yoku nai desu** (*isn't good*).

_____

★じゃ **ja** in negative forms can be では **de wa**.

Describing buildings

The following adjectives are useful for describing the appearance of buildings:

big	大きい	**ōkii**
low	低い	**hikui**
new	新しい	**atarashii**
old	古い	**furui**
small	小さい	**chīsai**
tall	高い	**takai**

Remember that 古い **furui** (*old*) is used only for things and not for people or animals to mean their age.

Describing rooms

The following adjectives are useful for describing a room:

bright	明るい	**akarui**
dark	暗い	**kurai**
dirty	汚い	**kitanai**
non-spacious (small)	せまい	**semai**
pretty/clean	きれいな	**kirei na**
quiet	しずかな	**shizuka na**
spacious	広い	**hiroi**

Encouraging someone to do something with どうぞ dōzo

どうぞ **dōzo** is an adverb used to encourage a person to do an action. It means *Please* or *Please go ahead and do (it)*. For example:

どうぞ入ってください。
Dōzo haitte kudasai.
Please come in.

どうぞ座ってください。
Dōzo suwatte kudasai.
Please sit down.

どうぞ受け取ってください。
Dōzo uketotte kudasai.
Please take (literally receive) it.

Often when you're encouraging someone to do something, you use gestures or hold out something to the person, so there's no need to complete the sentence: You can simply say どうぞ **dōzo**.

Entering your friend's house with おじゃまします ojamashimasu

When you enter someone's house or apartment room, say おじゃまします **ojamashimasu** as you walk in or right before you step in the room. Its literal meaning is *I will disturb you*, but it is understood as *I'm coming in!* rather than something negative.

EXERCISE
7·2

Write the phrase that means the opposite of each of the following, as shown in the example.

EXAMPLE   広いです **hiroi desu** (*is spacious*)

　　　　　せまいです **semai desu**

1. 新しいです **atarashii desu** (*is new*) _____

2. きれいです **kirei desu** (*is pretty*) _____

3. 低いです **hikui desu** (*is low*) _____

4. 暗いです **kurai desu** (*is dark*) _____

5. 小さいです **chīsai desu** (*is small*) _____

EXERCISE
7·3

Answer the following questions negatively, as shown in the example.

EXAMPLE   田中さんの部屋はきれいですか。

Tanaka-san no heya wa kirei desu ka.

Is Mr. Tanaka's room pretty?

いいえ, きれいじゃありません。**Īe, kirei ja arimasen.** *No, it is not pretty.*

1. 田中さんのアパートは新しいですか。

Tanaka-san no apāto wa atarashii desu ka.

Is Mr. Tanaka's apartment new?

_____

2. あのレストランは静かですか。

Ano resutoran wa shizuka desu ka.

Is that restaurant quiet?

_____

3. 寮の部屋は広いですか。

Ryō no heya wa hiroi desu ka.

Is the dormitory room big?

_____

Emiko is entering Alison's apartment for the first time. Complete their dialog with the appropriate words.

ALISON   ああ, 恵美子さん!どうぞ!

Ā, Emiko-san! Dōzo!

EMIKO   おじゃまします。

Ojamashimasu!

きれいな部屋ですね。

Kirei na heya desu ne.

ALISON   そうですか。

Sō desu ka.

EMIKO   ええ。_____ ですよ。それに広いですね。

Ē. _____ desu yo. Soreni hiroi desu ne.

ALISON   そうですか。

Sō desu ka.

Character of a person

This section introduces many useful adjectives for describing a person's character and personality. You will also learn degree adverbs that can be used along with them as well as question words that can ask about such properties.

Personality

The following adjectives are useful for describing a person's character and personality:

interesting/funny	面白い	omoshiroi
kind	やさしい	yasashii
lively	にぎやかな	nigiyaka na
quiet	静かな	shizuka na
scary	こわい	kowai
selfish	わがままな	wagamama na
sensitive	繊細な	sensai na
serious	まじめな	majime na
smart	頭がいい	atama ga ii
strict	厳しい	kibishii
thoughtful	親切な	shinsetsu na

Question words for state: どんな **donna** and どう **dō**

To ask the state of someone or something, use どんな **donna** (*what kind of*) or どう **dō** (*how*). Before a noun, use どんな **donna**; otherwise, use どう **dō**. For example:

新しいルームメートはどうですか。
Atarashii rūmumēto wa dō desu ka.
How is the new roommate?

新しいルームメートはどんな人ですか。
Atarashii rūmumēto wa donna hito desu ka.
What kind of person is the new roommate?

Adverbs of degree

Commonly used degree adverbs are listed here:

very much	とても	**totemo**
more or less	まあまあ	**māmā**
a little bit	ちょっと	**chotto**
not . . . very much	あまり	**amari**
not . . . at all	ぜんぜん	**zenzen**

あまり **amari** and ぜんぜん **zenzen** must be used with a negative form of an adjective, regardless of the meaning of the adjective. By contrast, ちょっと **chotto** and まあまあ **māmā** must be used with an affirmative form of an adjective, but ちょっと **chotto** must be used with an adjective that has an unpleasant or unfavorable meaning, and まあまあ **māmā** must be used with an adjective that has a pleasant or favorable meaning.

EXERCISE
7·5

For each of the following, choose the correct answer from the options in parentheses.

1. 田中さんの彼女は（どんな, どう）人ですか。

   Tanaka-san no kanojo wa (donna, dō) hito desu ka.

   What kind of person is Mr. Tanaka's girlfriend?

2. 新しいマネージャーは（どんな, どう）ですか。

   Atarashii manējā wa (donna, dō) desu ka.

   How is the new manager?

   （マネージャー **manējā** means *manager*）

3. （どんな, どう）人と結婚したいですか。

   (Donna, Dō) hito to kekkon-shi-tai desu ka.

   What kind of person do you want to get married to?

   （. . . と結婚する **to kekkon-suru** means *to get married to* . . .）

EXERCISE

7·6

Answer the following questions negatively, as shown in the example.

EXAMPLE   きれいですか。 **Kirei desu ka.** *Is (she) pretty?*

<u>いいえ, きれいじゃありません。</u>**Īe, kirei ja arimasen.**

1. 親切ですか。**Shinsetsu desu ka.** *Is (he/she) kind?*

_____

2. 優しいですか。**Yasashii desu ka.** *Is (he/she) kind?*

_____

3. まじめですか。**Majime desu ka.** *Is (he/she) serious?*

_____

4. 静かですか。**Shizuka desu ka.** *Is (he/she) quiet?*

_____

EXERCISE

7·7

For each of the following, choose the correct answer from the options in parentheses.

1. 父は（まあまあ, ちょっと）やさしいです。

   Chichi wa (māmā, chotto) yasashii desu.

2. 母は（ぜんぜん, ちょっと）こわくありません。

   Haha wa (zenzen, chotto) kowaku arimasen.

3. 兄は（まあまあ, ちょっと, あまり）わがままです。

   Ani wa (māmā, chotto, amari) wagamama desu.

4. 姉は（とても, あまり）まじめです。

   Ane wa (totemo, amari) majime desu.

EXERCISE

7·8

Describe the character of your family members as much as you can.

_____

_____

_____

_____

Appearance of a person

This section introduces useful adjectives for describing a person's appearance. You can describe a person very generally, as in *She is pretty,* or more specifically, as in *She has pretty eyes.* So, you need to know both ways.

Double subject

You may need to narrow down the scope of the adjective a little bit when describing someone's appearance. For example, say that you do not think a person is pretty in general, but you think she has beautiful eyes. In this case, say . . . は目がきれいです。 **wa me ga kirei desu**. It is as if there are two subjects: One is treated as the topic and is marked by は **wa**, and the other appears after it, with the particle が **ga**. For example, you can say:

美智子さんは目がきれいです。
Michiko-san wa me ga kirei desu.
Michiko has beautiful eyes.

The previous sentence has basically the same meaning as the following sentence:

美智子さんの目はきれいです。
Michiko-san no me wa kirei desu.
Michiko's eyes are pretty.

However, these two sentences differ in terms of what the speaker is talking about. The first one is about Michiko. The speaker is probably trying to describe what kind of person Michiko is. The second sentence is about Michiko's eyes. The speaker is talking about Michiko's eyes for some reason.

Words for describing the appearance of people

The appearance of people can sometimes be expressed using simple adjectives, but it may require a complex adjective phrase (. . . **wa** . . . **ga** . . . **desu**) or a complex verb phrase that ends in the auxiliary verb いる **iru**, even if the same state can be expressed by a single English word. (See Chapter 5 for more about the auxiliary verb いる **iru**.)

The following words and phrases are useful for describing someone's appearance:

overweight	太っている	**futotte iru**
has a long nose (literally, tall/high nose)	鼻が高い	**hana ga takai**
has a small nose (literally, low/flat nose)	鼻が低い	**hana ga hikui**
has a thick head of hair	髪が多い	**kami ga ōi**
has a thin head of hair	髪が少ない	**kami ga sukunai**
has big eyes	目が大きい	**me ga ōkii**
has long hair	髪が長い	**kami ga nagai**
has short hair	髪が短い	**kami ga mijikai**
has small eyes	目が小さい	**me ga chīsai**
pretty	きれいな	**kirei na**
short	背が低い	**se ga hikui**
skinny	やせている	**yasete iru**
tall	背が高い	**se ga takai**

Complete the following sentences appropriately.

1. 幸子さんは _____ です。

   Sachiko-san wa _____ desu.

   Sachiko is tall.

2. デイビッドさんは _____ 。

   Deibiddo-san wa _____ .

   David is skinny.

3. メアリーさんは _____ 。

   Mearī-san wa _____ .

   Mary has short hair.

4. ジョージさんは _____ 。

   Jōji-san wa _____ .

   George is short.

Describe the appearance of your family members as much as you can.

_____

_____

_____

_____

Choose the appropriate answer from the options in parentheses in the following dialog between George and Mike.

GEORGE　マイクさんの彼女は(どう, どんな, だれ)人ですか。

　　　　Maiku-san no kanojo wa (dō, donna, dare) hito desu ka.

MIKE　とても(やさしい, 広い, 狭い)人です。

　　　　Totemo (yasashii, hiroi, semai) hito desu.

GEORGE	きれいですか。
	Kirei desu ka.
MIKE	はい, (まあまあ, ちょっと)きれいです。
	Hai, (māmā, chotto) kirei desu.
GEORGE	ああ, そうですか。いいですね。
	Ā, sō desu ka. Ii desu ne.

Language learning

Here you'll learn how to describe learning. You'll learn how to express degree of difficulty, paying attention to specific aspects of learning in a variety of learning contexts. In addition, you'll learn the conjunctions それに **soreni** to provide a thorough and objective description of learning.

Expressing degree of difficulty with . . . にくい **nikui** and . . . やすい **yasui**

To say that something is difficult or easy to do, use the verb in the stem form (pre-**masu** form) and add にくい **nikui** if it is difficult or やすい **yasui** if it is easy. For example, 書きにくいです **kaki-nikui desu** means *it is difficult to write*, and 書きやすいです **kaki-yasui desu** means *it is easy to write*. The combination of the verb stem and にくい **nikui** or やすい **yasui** can be treated as a complex **i**-adjective. So, you can conjugate it just like an **i**-adjective. For example:

書きやすくありません。
Kaki-yasuku arimasen.
It is not easy to write.

これは書きやすい漢字ですね。
Kore wa kaki-yasui kanji desu ne.
This one is an easy-to-write kanji.

Words for describing courses

Some people learn languages in a classroom, and others learn by themselves, using books and audiovisual materials. To describe courses or learning experiences, use the following words and phrases:

conversation	会話	**kaiwa**
difficult	難しい	**muzukashii**
difficult to remember	覚えにくい	**oboe-nikui**
easy	簡単な	**kantan na**
exam	試験	**shiken**
has a lot of . . .	. . . が多い	**. . . ga ōi**
has little . . .	. . . が少ない	**. . . ga sukunai**
homework	宿題	**shukudai**
listening comprehension	聞き取り	**kiki-tori**
pronunciation	発音	**hatsuon**
quiz	小テスト	**shōtesuto**
reading and writing	読み書き	**yomi-kaki**

Do not use 多い **ōi** and 少ない **sukunai** as a modifier placed right before a noun (prenominal modifier). Rather, use them only at the end of the sentence, as a sentence predicates. For example, do not say 多い試験があります **Ōi shiken ga arimasu**, but say 試験が多いです **Shiken ga ōi desu** to mean *There are a lot of exams.*

The conjunction それに **soreni**

When you are providing additional information about the idea you've been talking about, use それに **soreni**. For example:

日本語は簡単です。 それに, 面白いです。
Nihongo wa kantan desu. Soreni, omoshiroi desu.
Japanese is easy. In addition, it is interesting.

To add information that contrasts with what you've been talking about, use でも **demo** instead of それに **soreni**. (See Chapter 5 for more about でも **demo**.)

EXERCISE 7·12

The following was written by Alison, who is taking Chinese and Japanese at her college. Read it and answer the questions that follow.

私は今大学で中国語のクラスと日本語のクラスをとっています。 中国語のクラスは宿題が多いです。 読み書きがとても難しいです。 それに先生が厳しいです。 でも試験が簡単です。 日本語のクラスも宿題が多いです。 漢字の小テストも多いです。 でも先生が優しいです。 それに試験が簡単です。

Watashi wa ima daigaku de Chūgokugo no kurasu to Nihongo no kurasu o totte imasu. Chūgokugo no kurasu wa shukudai ga ōi desu. Yomikaki ga totemo muzukashii desu. Soreni sensei ga kibishii desu. Demo, shiken ga kantan desu. Nihongo no kurasu mo shukudai ga ōi desu. Kanji no shōtesuto mo ōi desu. Demo sensei ga yasashii desu. Soreni shiken ga kantan desu.

1. Is there a lot of homework in Alison's Japanese class? _____

2. Are the exams in her Chinese class difficult? _____

3. Which course has a strict instructor? _____
   _____

EXERCISE 7·13

Complete the following sentences creatively, based on your own experience of studying Japanese.

日本語は _____ が難しいです。でも _____ が簡単です。

Nihongo wa _____ ga muzukashii desu. Demo _____ ga kantan desu.

Deciding on a travel destination

When deciding on where to travel, you will probably want to think about what you can see, what you can do, and what the weather is likely to be. Here you'll learn words and phrases that will help you talk about these things.

Sightseeing attractions

Here are some terms you might use to talk about the sightseeing options at a travel destination:

art museum	美術館	**bijutsukan**
forest	森	**mori**
hot spring	温泉	**onsen**
lake	湖	**mizuumi**
monument	記念碑	**kinenhi**
mountain	山	**yama**
ocean	海	**umi**
shrine	神社	**jinja**
ski area	スキー場	**sukījō**
temple	寺	**tera**
theater	劇場	**gekijō**

Description of places

Here are some terms you might use to describe a travel destination:

crowded and lively	にぎやかな	**nigiyaka na**
famous for . . .	で有名な . . .	**de yūmei na**
has a lot of . . .	が多い . . .	**ga ōi . . .**
has a pretty . . .	がきれいな . . .	**ga kirei na . . .**
has cheap . . .	が安い . . .	**ga yasui . . .**
has delicious . . .	がおいしい . . .	**ga oishii . . .**

Seasons and climates

Here are some terms you might use to talk about the seasons and climate of a travel destination:

cold	寒い	**samui**
cool	涼しい	**suzushii**
fall	秋	**aki**
hot	暑い	**atsui**
spring	春	**haru**
summer	夏	**natsu**
warm	暖かい	**atatakai**
winter	冬	**fuyu**

Listing examples with や ya

You can list some items as examples by using the particle や **ya**. Like と **to**, や **ya** can be used only with nouns. For example:

寺や神社があります。
Tera ya jinja ga arimasu.
There are things like temples and shrines.

シュノーケリングや水上スキーができます。
Shunōkeringu ya suijō-sukī ga dekimasu.
You can do snorkeling, water skiing, etc.

Places you may visit in Japan

Here are the names of some travel destinations in Japan:

Akihabara	秋葉原	**Akihabara**
Kyoto	京都	**Kyōto**
Nara	奈良	**Nara**
Okinawa	沖縄	**Okinawa**
Sapporo	札幌	**Sapporo**

EXERCISE
7·14

Read the following passage and answer the questions that follow.

北海道は食べ物がおいしいです。 温泉があります。 それにスキーもできます。 夏は涼しいです。 冬は寒いです。 でも冬は札幌で有名な雪祭りが見られます。 沖縄は海がきれいです。いつも暑いです。ですから, いつも泳げます。京都は古い寺や神社がたくさんあります。 東京と大阪は人が多いです。

Hokkaidō wa tabemono ga oishii desu. Onsen ga arimasu. Soreni sukī mo dekimasu. Natsu wa suzushii desu. Fuyu wa samui desu. Demo fuyu wa Sapporo de yūmei na yukimatsuri ga miraremasu. Okinawa wa umi ga kirei desu. Itsumo atsui desu. Desukara, itsumo oyogemasu. Kyōto wa furui tera ya jinja ga takusan arimasu. Tōkyō to Ōsaka wa hito ga ōi desu.

(食べ物 **tabemono** means *food*; 雪祭 **yuki matsuri** means *Snow Festival*)

1. What kind of place is Hokkaiddo?

   _____

2. Is it hot in Okinawa?

   _____

3. What sightseeing attractions will you find in Kyoto?

   _____

EXERCISE
7·15

Describe the places you have visited in the past.

_____

_____

_____

_____

Describing a meal at a restaurant

When talking about your experience of dining at a restaurant, you describe it with adjectives in the past tense. Here you'll learn how to form them, along with some terms that help you describe different cuisines and tastes.

Adjectives in the past tense

See how adjectives pattern in a past neutral-polite context in the following table:

	I Adjectives (e.g., 高い **takai** *expensive*)	Na Adjectives (e.g., 高価な **kōka na** *expensive*)
Affirmative	Stem + かったです Stem + **katta desu** 高かったです **takakatta desu** *was expensive*	Stem + でした Stem + **deshita** 高価でした **kōka deshita** *was expensive*
Negative	Stem + くありませんでした Stem + **ku arimasendeshita** *or* Stem +くなかったです Stem + **ku nakatta desu** 高くありませんでした **takaku arimasendeshita** 高くなかったです **takaku nakatta desu** *was not expensive*	Stem + じゃありませんでした Stem + **ja arimasendeshita** *or* Stem +じゃなかったです Stem + **ja nakatta desu** 高価じゃありませんでした **kōka ja arimasendeshita** 高価じゃなかったです **kōka ja nakatta desu** *was not expensive*

Words for ethnic cuisine

Here are some terms you might use to talk about ethnic cuisine:

Chinese cuisine	中華料理	**Chūka-ryōri**
French cuisine	フランス料理	**Furansu-ryōri**
Indian cuisine	インド料理	**Indo-ryōri**
Italian cuisine	イタリア料理	**Itaria-ryōri**
Japanese cuisine	日本料理	**Nihon-ryōri**
Korean cuisine	韓国料理	**Kankoku-ryōri**
Spanish cuisine	スペイン料理	**Supein-ryōri**
Thai cuisine	タイ料理	**Tai-ryōri**

Words for tastes

Here are some terms you might use to talk about tastes:

delicious	おいしい	**oishii**
bad taste	まずい	**mazui**
salty	塩辛い	**shiokarai**
sour	すっぱい	**suppai**
sweet	甘い	**amai**
bitter	苦い	**nigai**
spicy	辛い	**karai**
nice aroma	香りがいい	**kaori ga ii**

EXERCISE

7·16

Rewrite the following phrases in the past tense.

1. おいしいです **oishii desu** *is delicious* _____

2. まずいです **mazui desu** *is bad taste* _____

3. 甘いです **amai desu** *is sweet* _____

4. 塩辛いです **shiokarai desu** *is salty* _____

5. 香りがいいです **kaori ga ii desu** *has nice aroma* _____

EXERCISE

7·17

Rewrite the following phrases in the past tense.

1. おいしくありません **oishiku arimasen** _____

2. まずくありません **mazuku arimasen** _____

3. すっぱくありません **suppaku arimasen** _____

4. 苦くありません **nigaku arimasen** _____

5. 辛くありません **karaku arimasen** _____

EXERCISE

7·18

In the following dialog, Yukiko is telling Takeshi about her experience of dining at an Italian restaurant. Fill in the blanks in this dialog appropriately. Refer to Chapter 8 on . . . んです **n desu** *(It is the case that . . .).*

YUKIKO 昨日, 駅の近くの新しいイタリア料理のレストランに行ったんです。

Kinō, eki no chikaku no atarashii Itaria-ryōri no resutoran ni itta n desu.

TAKESHI ああ, そうですか。どうでしたか。

Ā, sō desu ka. Dō deshita ka.

YUKIKO まあまあおいし1. _____。

Māmā oishi 1. _____.

TAKESHI ああ, そうですか。高かったですか。

Ā, sō desu ka. Takakatta desu ka.

YUKIKO いいえ, あまり2. _____。

Īe, amari 2. _____.

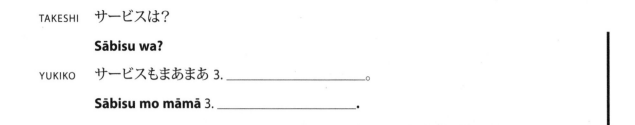

TAKESHI サービスは？

Sābisu wa?

YUKIKO サービスもまあまあ 3. _____。

Sābisu mo māmā 3. _____.

Preferences and skills

Here you will learn to express your preferences and your skills. You will learn how to indicate what you like and dislike and what you like or dislike doing. You'll learn what words to use to express preferences and to talk about a person's skills.

Indicating what you like and dislike with が ga

Unlike in English, in Japanese, preferences are usually expressed by adjectives although their English translations have a verb like *to like* and *to hate*. So, the item being liked or hated has to be marked by the particle が **ga** rather than を **o** because を **o** can be used only to mark the direct object noun of a verb. For example, if you like dogs, say:

私は犬が好きです。
Watashi wa inu ga suki desu.
I like dogs.

Words for preferences

The following words and phrases help you express preferences:

to hate	嫌いです（嫌いな）	kirai desu (kirai na)
to hate a lot	大嫌いです（大嫌いな）	daikirai desu (daikirai na)
to like	好きです（好きな）	suki desu (suki na)
to like a lot	大好きです（大好きな）	daisuki desu (daisuki na)

Nominalizing a verb with の no

To say that you like or dislike "doing" something, use the verb in the dictionary form and add の **no**. This makes the verb like a noun, and such a nominalized verb, or the sequence of the verb and の **no,** can be then marked by the particle が **ga** in a sentence that describes what one likes or dislikes. (こと **koto** may be used instead of の **no**, but の **no** is preferred for mentioning one's likes and dislikes.) For example:

私は食べるのが好きです。
Watashi wa taberu no ga suki desu.
I like eating.

Words for skills

To talk about a person's skills, use the following words and phrases:

to be good at	上手です（上手な）	jōzu desu (jōzu na)
to be good at and like . . .	得意です（得意な）	tokui desu (tokui na)
to be good at . . .	うまいです（うまい）	umai desu (umai)
to be bad at . . .	下手です（下手な）	heta desu (heta na)
to be bad at or hate . . .	苦手です（苦手な）	nigate desu (nigate na)

As with likes and dislikes, you can use が **ga** to mark the noun or to mark the nominalized verb with the particle の **no**. When expressing skills, it is better to use 得意です **tokui desu** than 上手です **jōzu desu** or うまいです **umai desu**. They all mean *to be good at*, but 得意です **tokui desu** is more subjective and has more emphasis on fondness than the other two. Accordingly, it helps you avoid sounding arrogant. For example:

> 私はテニスが得意です。
> **Watashi wa tenisu ga tokui desu.**
> *I'm good at tennis.*

> 私は車を修理するのが得意です。
> **Watashi wa kuruma o shūri suru no ga tokui desu.**
> *I'm good at repairing a car.*

EXERCISE
7·19

Translate the following sentences into English.

1. 私は野菜が嫌いです。でも姉は野菜が大好きです。

   Watashi wa yasai ga kirai desu. Demo ane wa yasai ga daisuki desu.

   _____

2. 山田さんはピアノを弾くのが上手です。

   Yamada-san wa piano o hiku no ga jōzu desu.

   _____

3. 兄は人と話すのが下手です。

   Ani wa hito to hanasu no ga heta desu.

   _____

4. 姉はテニスが得意です。毎朝友達とテニスをしています。

   Ane wa tenisu ga tokui desu. Maiasa tomodachi to tenisu o shite imasu.

   _____

EXERCISE
7·20

State what you like and dislike, as well as what you are good at and what you are not good at, in Japanese.

_____

_____

_____

_____

Saying what you want

There are a couple ways to express desire in Japanese: using ほしい **hoshii** and . . . たい **tai**.

Expressing desire with ほしい **hoshii**

To say what you want, use the adjective ほしい **hoshii** (*to want*) and mark the item with the particle が **ga**.

> 私は新しい車がほしいです。
> **Watashi wa atarashii kuruma ga hoshii desu.**
> *I want a new car.*

Expressing desire with . . . たい **tai**

To say what you want to do, create a complex adjective by adding たい **tai** (*to want to do . . .*) after the stem form (i.e., pre-**masu** form) of the verb. For example, the stem form of 飲む **nomu** (*drink*) is 飲み **nomi**, so by adding たい **tai**, you get 飲みたい **nomi-tai** (*want to drink*). The item is now marked by the particle that the original verb would assign, but if it is を **o**, it may be changed to が **ga**. The difference is very subtle. For example:

> ビールを飲みたいです。
> **Bīru o nomi-tai desu.**
> *I want to drink beer. (What I want to do is to drink beer.)*

> ビールが飲みたいです。
> **Bīru ga nomi-tai desu.**
> *I want to drink beer. (What I want to drink is beer.)*

Other particles stay the same. For example:

> 日本に行きたいです。
> **Nihon ni iki-tai desu.**
> *I want to go to Japan.*

EXERCISE 7·21

Read the following passage written by Minoru and answer the questions that follow.

僕は車がほしいです。 今は車がありません。 ですからいつも友達の車で大学に行っています。 とても不便です。 それから新しいスマートホンがほしいです。 今のは使いにくいです。 でもお金がありません。 今マクドナルドでバイトをしています。

Boku wa kuruma ga hoshii desu. Ima wa kuruma ga arimasen. Desukara itsumo tomodachi no kuruma de daigaku ni itte imasu. Totemo fuben desu. Sorekara atarashii sumātohon ga hoshii desu. Ima no wa tsukai-nikui desu. Demo o-kane ga arimasen. Ima Makudonarudo de baito o shite imasu.

(バイトをする **baito o suru** means *to work part-time*)

1. What are the two things Minoru wants to get now?

2. How does he commute to his college?

_____

3. Where does he work part time now?

_____

Clothing

When you go shopping for clothing, you describe it by using adjectives for attributes such as color and size. Here you'll learn such adjectives, as well as words for clothing and accessories, verbs for wearing, and how to talk about trying on clothes.

Words for colors

Colors in Japanese have different forms depending on whether they are used as nouns or modifiers. The following table shows these forms:

	USED AS A NOUN		USED AS A PRENOMINAL MODIFIER	
black	黒	kuro	黒い/黒の	kuroi/kuro no
blue	青	ao	青い/青の	aoi/ao no
brown	茶色	chairo	茶色い/茶色の	chairoi/chairo no
green	緑	midori	緑の	midori no
grey	灰色	haiiro	灰色の	haiiro no
orange	オレンジ	orenji	オレンジの	orenji no
pink	ピンク	pinku	ピンクの	pinku no
purple	紫	murasaki	紫の	murasaki no
red	赤	aka	赤い/赤の	akai/aka no
white	白	shiro	白い/白の	shiroi/shiro no
yellow	黄色	kiiro	黄色い/黄色の	kiiroi/kiiro no

Words for sizes

The following list gives some words for clothing size:

big	大きい	ōkii
small	小さい	chīsai
long	長い	nagai
short	短い	mijikai
size small	Sサイズ	esu saizu
size medium	Mサイズ	emu saizu
size large	Lサイズ	eru saizu

Descriptions of clothing

The following are some words that will help you describe clothing:

adult-like	大人っぽい	otonappoi
childish	子どもっぽい	kodomoppoi
conservative	地味な	jimi na
cool-looking	かっこいい	kakko ii
cute	かわいい	kawaii
elegant	エレガントな	ereganto na

flashy	派手な	hade na
lovely, refined	素敵な	suteki na
refined, nice taste	上品な	jōhin na

Showing excessiveness with . . . すぎる sugiru

To say *too*, as in *too small* or *too big*, add すぎる **sugiru** after the adjective in the stem form. For example:

このシャツは大きすぎます。
Kono shatsu wa ōki-sugimasu.
This shirt is too big.

You can also use すぎる **sugiru** for excessive actions, such as *ate too much*. Use a verb in the stem form in this case. For example:

洋服を買いすぎました。
Yōfuku o kai-sugimashita.
I bought too many clothes.

Words for clothing and accessories

The following are some words that refer to clothing and accessories:

belt	ベルト	beruto
bottoms in general	ズボン	zubon
caps and hats in general	帽子	bōshi
coat	コート	kōto
dress	ドレス	doresu
jacket	ジャケット	jaketto
jeans	ジーパン	jīpan
necktie	ネクタイ	nekutai
shirt	シャツ	shatsu
shoes	靴	kutsu
skirt	スカート	sukāto
sneakers	スニーカー	sunīkā
socks	靴下	kutsushita
suit	スーツ	sūtsu
sunglasses	サングラス	sangurasu
sweater	セーター	sētā

The term ズボン **zubon** is not a fashionable term in modern Japanese, but it is still used as a generic term that refers to all sorts of bottoms, including the bottoms of pajamas and sweat suits. Alternatives include スラックス **surakkusu** (*slacks*), トラウザーズ **torauzāzu** (*trousers*), and パンツ **pantsu** (*pants*).

Verbs for wearing

The Japanese use different verbs to mean *to put on* or *to wear*. For items below the waist, such as pants, skirts, socks, and shoes, use 履く **haku**. For items for your head, such as caps and hats, use かぶる **kaburu**. For accessories such as necklaces, eyeglasses, earrings, watches, and belts, use する **suru**. For eyeglasses, かける **kakeru** is also possible. For other clothing items, such as jackets, dresses, kimonos, and shirts, use 着る **kiru**. Use all these verbs in the . . . ている **te iru** construction once the item is worn. (See Chapter 5 for the . . . ている **te iru** construction.) For example:

あの人は素敵なコートを着ていますね。
Ano hito wa suteki na kōto o kite imasu ne.
That person is wearing a nice coat, isn't he?

Trying on clothing: . . . みる **miru**

To express doing something as a trial, you use the verb in the te form and add the auxiliary verb みる **miru** (*to see*). For example:

> 着てみます
> **kite mimasu**
> *to try putting on some clothes*

Polite shop language: ございます **gozaimasu**

At stores, sales representatives use very polite business-like language. For example, they say ございます **gozaimasu** as opposed to あります **arimasu** to mean *We have*. As in:

> Mサイズは黒がございます。
> **Emu-saizu wa kuro ga gozaimasu.**
> *We have one black (item) in medium.*

EXERCISE 7·22

Write your favorite colors and the favorite colors of your family members.

EXAMPLE　　私は赤が好きです。　**Watashi wa aka ga suki desu.** *I like red.*

_____

_____

_____

_____

EXERCISE 7·23

In each of the following, choose the appropriate answer from the options in parentheses.

1. ジャケットを(着て, はいて, かぶって, して)います。

   Jaketto o (kite, haite, kabutte, shite) imasu.

   (She) is wearing a jacket.

2. スニーカーを(着て, はいて, かぶって, して)います。

   Sunīkā o (kite, haite, kabutte, shite) imasu.

   (She) is wearing sneakers.

3. 帽子を（着て，はいて，かぶって，して）います。

Bōshi o (kite, haite, kabutte, shite) imasu.

(She) is wearing a hat.

4. ネックレスを（着て，はいて，かぶって，して）います。

Nekkuresu o (kite, haite, kabutte, shite) imasu.

(She) is wearing a necklace.

Translate the following sentences into Japanese.

1. *This coat is too long.*

_____

2. *This dress is too conservative.*

_____

3. *This necklace is too expensive.*

_____

Translate the following sentences into Japanese.

1. *I like black and red.*

_____

2. *I tried this dress.*

_____

3. *Please try this skirt.*

_____

4. *I bought too many sweaters.*

_____

Read the following dialog between Mary and a sales representative at a store and translate the underlined parts.

MARY　すみません。このジャケットの黒はありますか。

Sumimasen. Kono jaketto no kuro wa arimasu ka.

SALES
REPRESENTATIVE　1. <u>あのう，黒はございません。緑はございます。</u>

1. <u>**Anō, kuro wa gozaimasen. Midori wa gozaimasu.**</u>

_____

MARY　緑ですか。

Midori desu ka.

SALES
REPRESENTATIVE　赤もございますよ。

Aka mo gozaimasu yo.

MARY　赤?

Aka?

SALES
REPRESENTATIVE　赤はかわいいですよ。2. <u>着てみてください。</u>

Aka wa kawaii desu yo. 2. <u>Kite mite kudasai.</u>

_____

MARY　3. <u>でも, これはちょっと小さすぎます。</u> L サイズはありますか。

3. <u>**Demo, kore wa chotto chīsa-sugimasu.**</u> **Eru-saizu wa arimasu ka.**

_____

Adverbs

Whereas adjectives describe things and people (nouns), adverbs describe manners of actions (verbs). For example, ゆっくり **yukkuri** (*slowly*) is an adverb. There are many adverbs that were derived from adjectives.

Adverbs derived from adjectives

In English you can turn an adjective into an adverb by adding *-ly*. Similarly, in Japanese, you can create adverbs from adjectives by adding に **ni** to the stem of a **na** adjective as in 静かに **shizuka ni** (*quietly*), or by adding く**ku** to the stem of an **i** adjective as in 早く **hayaku** (*quickly*). The adverb version of いい **ii** is よく **yoku**.

The adverb + する suru

If you use する **suru** (*do*) after an adverb, it means to change something or someone in a certain way. For example, 部屋をきれいにする **heya o kirei ni suru** means *to make the room clean* and 静かにする **shizuka ni suru** means *to make oneself quiet*. It is often used with もう少し **mō sukoshi** (*a little bit*) to ask someone to make some change.

EXERCISE 7·27

Convert the following adjectives into adverbs.

1. 上手な **jōzu na** (*skillful*) _____

2. 静かな **shizuka na** (*quiet*) _____

3. 早い **hayai** (*early*) _____

4. まじめな **majima na** (*serious*) _____

5. いい **ii** (*good*) _____

EXERCISE 7·28

Translate the following sentences into English.

1. ちょっとうるさいですよ。もう少し静かに勉強してください。

   Chotto urusai desu yo. Mō sukoshi shizuka ni benkyō shite kudasai.

   _____

2. 読めません。きれいに書いてください。それからもう少し大きく書いてください。

   Yomemasen. Kirei ni kaite kudasai. Sorekara mō sukoshi ōkiku kaite kudasai.

   _____

3. クラスは 9 時からです。もう少し早く来てください。

   Kurasu wa ku-ji kara desu. Mō sukoshi hayaku kite kudasai.

   _____

4. よく考えました。でもこの仕事はしないつもりです。

   Yoku kangaemashita. Demo kono shigoto wa shinai tsumori desu.

   _____

   (考える **kangaeru** means *to think about*)

5. もう少しまじめにしてください。

   Mō sukoshi majime ni shite kudasai.

   _____

Translate the following sentences into Japanese.

1. *Could you be quiet, please?*

   _____

2. *Could you make the room clean?*

   _____

3. *Could you come here early tomorrow?*

   _____

4. *Please read it carefully.*

   _____

Comparisons

In Japanese as in English, a number of comparisons are possible. Here you'll learn to compare two items to each other and to compare multiple items in the same group or category.

Comparing two items to each other

To say *A is more . . . than B*, just add B より **B yori** (*than* B) in the statement sentence that says *A is . . . .* For example:

> 犬はかわいいです。
> **Inu wa kawaii desu.**
> *Dogs are cute.*

> 犬は猫よりかわいいです。
> **Inu wa neko yori kawaii desu.**
> *Dogs are cuter than cats.*

To ask a question that involves comparing two items, such as *Which is more . . . , X or Y?* place XとYと **X to Y to**, at the beginning of the sentence and use どちらの方 **dochira no hō** (*which one*) to create a question sentence. For example:

> 犬と猫と, どちらの方がかわいいですか。
> **Inu to neko to, dochira no hō ga kawaii desu ka.**
> *Which are cuter, dogs or cats?*

Equivalent-degree comparisons

To show equivalence, use . . . と 同じぐらい . . . **to onaji gurai** (*as . . . as . . .*). For example, 犬はねこと同じぐらいかわいいです **Inu wa neko to onaji gurai kawaii desu** means *Dogs are as cute as cats*. By contrast, to express non-equivalence, use the particle ほど **hodo** (*(not as . . .) as*) along with a negative adjective or verb. For example:

> 犬は猫ほどかわいくありません 。
> **Inu wa neko hodo kawaiku arimasen,**
> *Dogs are not as cute as cats.*

Superlative comparisons

To express the superlative comparison, use the adverb 一番 **ichiban**, which literally means *the first*, *the best*, or *the most*. For example:

母が一番優しいです 。
Haha ga ichiban yasashii desu.
My mom is the kindest.

If the basis of superlative comparison is a list of items, list them, as in XとYとZの中で **X to Y to Z no naka de** or XとYとZとで **X to Y to Z to de**. For a class of items, add の中で **no naka de** after the name of the class. For example:

猫と犬と兎の中で猫が一番好きです。
Neko to inu to usagi no naka de neko ga ichiban suki desu.
Among cats, dogs, and rabbits, I like cats the best.

動物の中で猫が一番好きです。
Dōbutsu no naka de nekko ga ichiban suki desu.
Among animals, I like cats the best.

For superlative questions, never use どちら **dochira** (*which one*) because it is only used for comparing two items. Instead, use regular question words such as だれ **dare** (*who*), どこ **doko** (*where*), いつ **itsu** (*when*), and 何 **nani** (*what*). But note that 何 **nani** is replaced with どれ **dore** (*which one*) if the question is based on a list of items rather than a class of items. For example:

果物の中で何が一番好きですか。
Kudamono no naka de nani ga ichiban suki desu ka.
Among fruit, what do you like the best?

桃と苺とりんごの中でどれが一番好きですか。
Momo to ichigo to ringo no naka de dore ga ichiban suki desu ka.
Among peaches, strawberries, and apples, which do you like the best?

Words for classes of items

These are some words that will help you describe classes of items:

animals	動物	**dōbutsu**
beverages	飲み物	**nomimno**
buildings	建物	**tatemono**
colors	色	**iro**
flowers	花	**hana**
foods	食べ物	**tabemono**
fruits	果物	**kudamono**
meats	肉	**niku**
pets	ペット	**petto**
sports	スポーツ	**supōtsu**
subjects (academic)	教科	**kyōka**
vegetables	やさい	**yasai**

EXERCISE

7·30

Complete each of the following sentences with the appropriate word or phrase.

1. 犬と猫と, _____ が好きですか。

   Inu to neko to, _____ ga suki desu ka.

   Which do you like better, dogs or cats?

2. クラスの中で _____ が一番よく勉強しますか。

   Kurasu no naka de _____ ga ichiban yoku benkyō shimasu ka.

   Who studies the most in class?

3. 動物の中で _____ が一番好きですか。

   Dōbutsu no naka de _____ ga ichiban suki desu ka.

   Among animals, what do you like the best?

4. 犬と猫と兎の中で _____ が一番好きですか。

   Inu to neko to usagi no naka de _____ ga ichiban suki desu ka.

   Which do you like the best among dogs, cats, and rabbits?

5. 犬は猫 _____ かわいいですよ。

   Inu wa neko _____ kawaii desu yo.

   Dogs are cuter than cats.

6. 犬は猫 _____ かわいくありませんよ。

   Inu wa neko _____ kawaiku arimasen yo.

   Dogs are not as cute as cats.

7. 犬は猫 _____ かわいいですよ。

   Inu wa neko _____ kawaii desu yo.

   Dogs are as cute as cats.

EXERCISE

7·31

Answer the following questions in Japanese.

1. 果物の中で何が一番好きですか。

   Kudamono no naka de nani ga ichiban suki desu ka.

   Among fruits, what do you like the best?

2. スポーツの中で何を一番よくしますか。

Supōtsu no naka de nani o ichiban yoku shimasu ka.

Among sports, what do you play the most?

_____

3. すしとさしみと，どちらの方が好きですか。

Sushi to sashimi to, dochira no hō ga suki desu ka.

Between sushi and sashimi, which one do you like better?

_____

4. 日本料理と中華料理と韓国料理の中でどれが一番好きですか。

Nihon-ryōri to Chūka-ryōri to Kankoku-ryōri no naka de dore ga ichiban suki desu ka.

Among Japanese cuisine, Chinese cuisine, and Korean cuisine, which do you like the best?

_____

**EXERCISE
7·32**

Translate the following sentences into Japanese.

1. *My father is not as kind as my mother.*

_____

2. *Which is easier, Chinese or Japanese?*

_____

3. *Which is safer: cars or planes?*

(安全な **anzen na** means *safe*)

_____

4. *Katakana is as easy as hiragana.*

_____

5. *I'm taller than my father.*

_____

Making connections

In this chapter, you will learn how to make connections by relating facts and your thoughts in order to communicate coherently and effectively. You'll learn to make connections in a number of ways, such as stating what you think, sharing experiences, and using conjunctions.

Stating what you think with 思います omoimasu

Here you will learn how to use the quotation particle と **to** to express what you think. You will also learn how to create **ta** forms of verbs and adjectives, which you need to use to express past events in this construction.

The quotation particle と **to**

At the end of a statement, you can add *that's what I think* by using the verb 思う **omou** (*think*) along with the particle と **to**. と **to** marks what is being quoted and can be used when the main verb is 聞きました **kikimashita** (*I heard*) or 言いました **iimashita** (*I said*) or 思います **omoimasu** (*I think*). For example:

> 兄は数学は簡単だと言いました。
> **Ani wa sūgaku wa kantan da to iimashita.**
> *My older brother said that math is easy.*

> 私はジョージさんはイギリスに帰ったと聞きました。
> **Watashi wa Jōji-san wa Igirisu ni kaetta to kikimashita.**
> *I heard that George returned to England.*

> 私はこの本は安いと思います。
> **Watashi wa kono hon wa yasui to omoimasu.**
> *I think this book is cheap.*

For stating a third person's thinking, use 思っています **omotte imasu** instead of 思います **omoimasu**. For example:

> 父は私は頭がよくないと思っています。
> **Chichi wa watashi wa atama ga yokunai to omotte imasu.**
> *My father thinks that I am not smart.*

Plain forms in the non-past tense

Before the quotation particle と **to**, the verbs and adjectives need to be in the plain form unless they are a part of a direct quote. The plain past affirmative forms are also called **ta forms** because they all end in た **ta** (or sometimes だ **da**). The **ta** form of a verb is very easy to make if you already know a **te** form: Just change the vowel **e** at the end of the **te** form to **a**. For example, the **te** form of 食べる **taberu** (*eat*) is 食べて **tabete**, and its **ta** form is 食べた **tabeta**. Similarly, the **te** form of 飲む **nomu** (*drink*) is 飲んで **nonde**, and its **ta** form is 飲んだ **nonda**. (See Chapter 5 for how to make the **te** form.)

The plain forms of verbs and adjectives, both non-past and past, both affirmative and negative, are summarized in the following table. To create a form, check the category or class of the item and follow the pattern of one of the items in this table:

	NON-PAST		PAST	
	AFFIRMATIVE	NEGATIVE	AFFIRMATIVE	NEGATIVE
Verbs	食べる **taberu** *will eat, eat, eats*	食べない **tabenai** *won't eat, doesn't/don't eat*	食べた **tabeta** *ate*	食べなかった **tabenakatta** *didn't eat*
Noun + Copula	犬だ **inu da** *is a dog*	犬じゃない **inu ja nai** *isn't a dog*	犬だった **inu datta** *was a dog*	犬じゃなかった **inu ja nakatta** *wasn't a dog*
Na adjective	高価だ **kōka da** *is expensive*	高価じゃない **kōka ja nai** *isn't expensive*	高価だった **kōka datta** *was expensive*	高価じゃなかった **kōka ja nakatta** *wasn't expensive*
I adjective	高い **takai** *is expensive*	高くない **takaku nai** *isn't expensive*	高かった **takakatta** *was expensive*	高くなかった **takaku nakatta** *wasn't expensive*

EXERCISE
8·1

Convert the following verbs and adjectives in the polite form into the plain form.

1. 行きます **ikimasu** *will go* _____

2. 飲みました **nomimashita** *drank* _____

3. 食べませんでした **tabemasendeshita** *didn't eat* _____

4. 高かったです **takakatta desu** *was expensive* _____

5. きれいでした **kirei deshita** *was pretty* _____

6. すしじゃありませんでした **sushi ja arimasendeshita** *wasn't sushi* _____

Convert the following verbs and adjectives from the polite form into the plain form. These verbs and adjectives are slightly complex because they include auxiliary verbs or suffixes.

1. 飲んでいました **nonde imashita** *was drinking* _____

2. 飲めません **nomemasen** *is not able to drink* _____

3. 読みたいです **yomi-tai desu** *want to read* _____

4. 食べすぎました **tabe-sugimashita** *ate too much* _____

5. 着てみます **kite mimasu** *will try it on* _____

Translate the following sentences into Japanese.

1. *I think Japanese is easy.*

_____

2. *I think I cannot write kanji. (I don't think I can write kanji.)*

_____

3. *I think this sweater is too big.*

_____

4. *I think the food at that restaurant was delicious.*

_____

5. *My mother thinks this dress is too expensive.*

_____

Using a relative clause

More than just adjectives can modify nouns in Japanese. You can use a noun to modify a noun with the help of the particle の **no**. You can use a verb to modify a noun if it is in the plain form and placed before the noun. You can even modify a noun by using a sentence that ends in a verb in the plain form.

For example, in the following sentence, the noun 映画 **eiga** (*movie*) is modified by a sentence marked by a pair of brackets, which means *I watched (the movie) yesterday* in the plain form:

[昨日私が見た]映画は面白かったです。
[Kinō watashi ga mita] eiga wa omoshirokatta desu.
The movie I watched yesterday was interesting.

This sentence, marked by a pair of brackets, does not actually say *the movie*. When you use a sentence with a gap like this before a noun with which the gap should be filled, we call it a *relative clause*. So, it's very useful to know plain forms even if you are speaking in a polite context.

EXERCISE 8·4

Reorder the items in each of the following sets to form a grammatical sentence.

1. 男の人は **otoko no hito wa** *the man* (topic marker), 来た **kita** *came*, 日本人でした **Nihonjin deshita** *was Japanese*, 昨日 **kinō** *yesterday*

_____

_____

_____

2. おいしかったです **oishikatta desu** *was delicious*, 母が **haha ga** *my mother* (subject marker), てんぷら **tenpura** *tempura*, 作った **tsukutta** *made*, は **wa** (topic marker)

_____

_____

_____

3. 田中さん **Tanaka-san** *Mr. Tanaka*, 昨日 **kinō** *yesterday*, 洋服を **yōfuku o** *clothing* (direct object marker), 今日も **kyō mo** *today also*, は **wa** (topic marker), 着ていた **kite ita** (*was wearing*), 着ています **kite imasu** (*am wearing*)

_____

_____

_____

EXERCISE 8·5

Translate the following sentences into Japanese.

1. The person who is drinking coffee over there is my friend.

_____

2. The car I bought last year is not good.

_____

3. That dog is the dog I saw in the park last week.

_____

Using . . . んです **n desu** for making connections in conversation

What you say in conversation is usually related to what was said or what you would like the other person to respond to. Otherwise, your speech will be disconnected from the context and your conversation partner will not fully understand why you are saying things you are saying. It is as if there is a hidden string that connects all utterances made by you and your conversation partner. To make such a tie stronger, the Japanese often end their sentences with んです . . . **n desu** in conversation. It may be to show that a statement is a part of the explanation to the previous utterance, implying *That's why*, or it may be to elicit the conversation partner's response, implying *What do you think? Any comment?*

So, んです **n desu** is a discourse tool for Japanese. It is actually the reduced form of のです **no desu**. It cannot be translated into English. It follows verbs and adjectives in the plain form except that the non-past affirmative copular verb だ **da** must be realized as な **na**. For example, to mean that you hate composition, if you say 私は作文が嫌いなんです **Watashi wa sakubun ga kirai na n desu** instead of 私は作文が嫌いです **Watashi wa sakubun ga kirai desu**, you can avoid sounding like a robot or sounding very blunt and harsh, and your conversation partner will naturally feel like responding to you with his/her comments and thoughts. Similarly, consider a scenario where your friend just saw you carrying a suitcase and appeared to be puzzled about it. Even before she asks you, you can say ハワイに行くんです **Hawai ni iku n desu** (*I'm going to Hawaii.*). Then your friend will know that you are trying to explain rather than abruptly making a statement. Therefore, there is no need to use んです **n desu** when you are writing or when you are giving a speech in front of an audience. んです **n desu** is a discourse tool that helps conversation participants engage in a smooth two-way communicative interaction.

EXERCISE
8·6

Rephrase the following sentences using んです **n desu**.

1. 来月結婚します。

   Raigetsu kekkon shimasu.

   I'll get married next month.

   _____

2. お金がありません。

   O-kane ga arimasen.

   I don't have money.

   _____

3. 会社を辞めました。

   Kaisha o yamemashita.

   I quit the company.

   _____

4. 私の父は韓国人です。

Watashi no chichi wa kankoku-jin desu.

My father is a Korean.

Asking "why?"

Next you will learn how to ask for a reason and how to state a reason. You'll also learn how to talk about possible reasons for studying Japanese.

Asking for a reason with どうして **dōshite**

To ask for a reason, say どうして **dōshite**, state the fact for which you are asking for the reason (in the plain form), and add んですか **n desu ka** at the end. Because you are using んです **n desu**, discussed in the previous section, make sure to change the non-past affirmative copula だ **da** to な **na**. For example:

> どうして田中さんが嫌いなんですか。
> **Dōshite Tanaka-san ga kirai na n desu ka.**
> *Why do you hate Mr. Tanaka?*

なんで **nande** also means *why*, but it is slightly informal and can also mean *by what* and so it can be ambiguous. なぜ **naze** also means *why*, but it is most appropriate for written form.

Stating a reason with からです **kara desu**

To answer a question with どうして **dōshite** (*why*), you can state the reason in the plain form and add からです **kara desu** at the end. For example:

> A: どうして田中さんが嫌いなんですか。
> **Dōshite Tanaka-san ga kirai na n desu ka.**
> *Why do you hate Mr. Tanaka?*

> B: 田中さんはうそつきだからです。
> **Tanaka-san wa usotsuki da kara desu.**
> *Because Mr. Tanaka is a liar.*

Possible reasons for studying Japanese

If you are studying Japanese, you will often be asked why you are doing so. The following are common reasons for studying Japanese:

I am interested in business.	ビジネスに興味がある。	**Bizinesu ni kyōmi ga aru.**
I have a Japanese friend.	日本人の友達がいる。	**Nihon-jin no tomodachi ga iru.**
I like anime and manga.	アニメとマンガが好きだ。	**Anime to manga ga sukida.**
I like Japanese culture.	日本の文化が好きだ。	**Nihon no bunka ga sukida.**
I like karate and kendo.	空手と剣道が好きだ。	**Karate to kendō ga sukida.**
I want to teach English in Japan.	日本で英語を教えたい。	**Nihon de eigo o oshie-tai.**
I want to work in Japan.	日本で働きたい。	**Nihon de hataraki-tai.**
Japanese language is very different from English.	日本語は英語とぜんぜん違う。	**Nihongo wa eigo to zenzen chigau.**

Following the example, create a question that asks the reason for each statement.

EXAMPLE   ボストンに行きます。

Bosuton ni ikimasu.

I will go to Boston.

<u>どうしてボストンに行くんですか。</u> **Dōshite Bosuton ni iku n desu ka**. *Why will*

<u>*you go to Boston?*</u>

1. ホテルをキャンセルしました。

Hoteru o kyanseru shimashita.

I cancelled the hotel (reservation).

_____

_____

2. 会議に出ません。

Kaigi ni demasen.

I will not attend the conference.

_____

_____

3. 山田さんの車を買いませんでした。

Yamada-san no kuruma o kaimasendeshita.

I did not buy Ms. Yamada's car.

_____

_____

4. 韓国語を勉強しています。

Kankokugo o benkyō shite imasu.

I'm studying Korean.

_____

_____

Following the example, create a sentence that causes the statement given to serve as a reason.

EXAMPLE   ボストンに行きます。

Bosuton ni ikimasu.

I will go to Boston.

<u>ボストンに行くからです。</u>   **Bosuton ni iku kara desu**. *It is because I will go to Boston.*

1. 漢字が難しいです。

Kanji ga muzukashii desu.

Kanji are hard.

_____

_____

2. お金がありません。

O-kane ga arimasen.

I don't have money.

_____

_____

3. とても高かったです。

Totemo takakatta desu.

It was very expensive.

_____

_____

4. あまりきれいじゃありませんでした。

Amari kirei ja arimasendeshita.

It was not very pretty.

_____

_____

EXERCISE
8·9

Answer the following question in Japanese, based on your personal situation.

どうして日本語を勉強しているんですか。

Dōshite Nihongo o benkyō shite iru n desu ka.

Why are you studying Japanese?

_____

_____

_____

Sharing experiences

Here you will learn how to talk about experiences. You'll learn the form you need to use as well as some words and phrases that will help you talk about your experiences.

Expressing experience with ことがあります koto ga arimasu

In order to express what experience you have, don't use a simple past sentence, but instead use ことがあります **koto ga arimasu**. **Arimasu** (*to exist, to have*) is in the non-past tense because you *have* the experience now. こと **koto** is an abstract noun that means *thing, occasion, matter*, etc. So, what you are literally saying is *I have the occasion of completing such and such*. Importantly, the verb before **koto** must be in the **ta** form (the plain past tense). For example:

私は納豆を食べたことがあります。 でも梅干を食べたことはありません。
Watashi wa nattō o tabeta koto ga arimasu. Demo, umeboshi o tabeta koto wa arimasen.
I have had fermented soybeans. However, I have never had pickled plum.

Experiences you might have

The following are the words for some experiences you might want to talk about:

to skydive	スカイダイビングをする	sukaidaibingu o suru
to eat fermented soybeans	納豆を食べる	nattō o taberu
to go to Europe	ヨーロッパに行く	Yōroppa ni iku
to go to karaoke	カラオケに行く	karaoke ni iku
to have a fight	喧嘩をする	kenka o suru
to lose a credit card	クレジットカードをなくす	kurejitto kādo o nakusu
to see Mt. Fuji	富士山を見る	Fujisan o miru
to stay in a traditional Japanese style-inn	旅館に泊まる	ryokan ni tomaru
to take a helicopter	ヘリコプターに乗る	herikoputā ni noru
to take Shinkansen (bullet train)	新幹線に乗る	Shinkansen ni noru
to watch kabuki play	歌舞伎を見る	kabuki o miru
to watch movies directed by Akira Kurosawa	黒澤明の映画を見る	Kurosawa Akira no eiga o miru
to wear a kimono	着物を着る	kimono o kiru

The counter 回 **kai** (. . . *times*)

To say *once, twice, three times*, etc., use the counter 回 **kai**. For example:

日本には3回行ったことがあります。
Nihon ni wa san-kai itta koto ga arimasu.
I've been to Japan three times.

The following table shows how to read this counter with numerals:

1回	2回	3回	4回	5回	6回	7回	8回	9回	10回
いっかい	にかい	さんかい	よんかい	ごかい	ろっかい	ななかい	はっかい／はちかい	きゅうかい	じゅっかい／じっかい
ik-kai	ni-kai	san-kai	yon-kai	go-kai	rok-kai	nana-kai	hak-kai/ hachi-kai	kyū-kai	juk-kai/ jik-kai

EXERCISE
8·10

Translate the following sentences into Japanese.

1. *Have you ever been to Japan?*

_____

2. *Have you ever lost your credit card before?*

_____

3. *Have you ever been in a helicopter?*

_____

4. *Have you watched Hayao Miyazaki's anime?*

_____

EXERCISE
8·11

Answer the questions from Exercise 8-10 in Japanese.

1. _____
2. _____
3. _____
4. _____

Read the following dialog between Justin and Mike and translate the underlined parts.

JUSTIN   1. <u>マイクさんは日本に行ったことがありますか。</u>

           1. Maiku-san wa Nihon ni itta koto ga arimasu ka.

_____

MIKE   はい, ありますよ。3回あります。

           Hai, arimasu yo. San-kai arimasu.

JUSTIN   カプセルインに泊まったことはありますか。

           Kapuseru-in ni tomatta koto wa arimasu ka.

MIKE   ありません。でも僕の友達は泊まったことがあります。

           Arimasen. Demo boku no tomodachi wa tomatta koto ga arimasu.

JUSTIN   ああ, そうですか。

           Ā, sō desu ka.

MIKE   2. <u>とても小さかったと言っていました。</u>

           2. Totemo chīsakatta to itte imashita.

_____

JUSTIN   3. <u>僕も泊まってみたいと思っているんです。</u>

           3. Boku mo tomatte mi-tai to omotte iru n desu.

_____

MIKE   ああ, そうですか。

           Ā, sō desu ka.

           (カプセルイン **kapuseru-in** means *capsule inn*, an inexpensive business hotel with extremely small rooms where one can barely sit up)

Forecasting weather

Next you will learn how to express probability. You will also learn words related to weather and how to talk about weather forecasting.

Expressing probability with でしょう **deshō**

When you think something is probably the case, make a statement in the plain form and add でしょう **deshō** at the end. Remember to drop the non-past affirmative copula だ **da**. For example:

> あしたは大雪でしょう。
> **Ashita wa ōyuki deshō.**
> *It will probably snow a lot tomorrow.*

Words for weather

The following words and phrases will help you talk about weather:

clear weather (sky)	晴れ	**hare**
cloud	雲	**kumo**
cloudy weather (sky)	曇り	**kumori**
drizzle	小雨	**kosame**
heavy rain	大雨	**ōame**
heavy snow	大雪	**ōyuki**
rain	雨	**ame**
snow	雪	**yuki**
storm	嵐	**arashi**
strong wind	強風	**kyōfū**
thunderstorm	雷雨	**raiu**
to become clear (sky)	晴れる	**hareru**
to become cloudy	曇る	**kumoru**
to fall	降る	**furu**
tornado	竜巻	**tatsumaki**
typhoon	台風	**taifū**
wind	風	**kaze**

EXERCISE

8·13

Translate the following sentences into English.

1. 今日は一日曇りでしょう。

   Kyō wa ichinichi kumori deshō.

   _____

2. 明日の午後は雨が降るでしょう。

   Ashita no gogo wa ame ga furu deshō.

   _____

3. 明日の晩は雪が降るでしょう。

   Ashita no ban wa yuki ga furu deshō.

   _____

4. 週末は晴れるでしょう。

   Shūmatsu wa hareru deshō.

   _____

Talking about sickness

Here you will learn how to talk about possibilities. You will also learn vocabulary words related to sickness and how to talk about symptoms and diagnoses.

Talking about a possible case with かもしれません kamoshiremasen

When you think something is possibly the case, make a statement in the plain form and add かもしれません kamoshiremasen (*It is possible that . . .*) at the end. Just remember to drop the non-past affirmative copula だ da. For example:

風邪かもしれません。
Kaze kamoshiremasen.
It may be a cold.

熱があるかもしれません。
Netsu ga aru kamoshiremasen.
I may have a fever.

仕事に行けないかもしれません。
Shigoto ni ikenai kamoshiremasen.
I may not be able to go to work.

Symptoms of illness

In case you need to go see a doctor in Japan, learn the following words and phrases:

to cough	咳が出る	**seki ga deru**
to have a fever	熱がある	**netsu ga aru**
to have a headache	頭が痛い	**atama ga itai**
to have a runny nose	鼻水が出る	**hanamizu ga deru**
to have a sore throat	喉が痛い	**nodo ga itai**
to have a stomachache	おなかが痛い	**onaka ga itai**
to have a stuffy nose	鼻がつまっている	**hana ga tsumatte iru**
to have constipation	便秘をしている	**benpi o shite iru**
to have diarrhea	下痢をしている	**geri o shite iru**
to have dizziness	目眩がする	**memai ga suru**
to have nausea	吐き気がする	**hakike ga suru**
to have phlegm	痰が出る	**tan ga deru**
to have the chills	寒気がする	**samuke ga suru**
to sneeze	くしゃみが出る	**kushami ga deru**
to wheeze	ゼーゼーする	**zē zē suru**

Diagnosis of illness

The following are words for common illnesses and injuries:

allergies	アレルギー	**arerugī**
appendicitis	盲腸	**mōchō**
arthritis	関節炎	**kansetsuen**
asthma	喘息	**zensoku**
broken bone	骨折	**kossetsu**
bronchitis	気管支炎	**kikanshien**
cancer	癌	**gan**
cold	風邪	**kaze**

food poisoning	食中毒	**shokuchūdoku**
influenza/flu	インフルエンザ	**infuruenza**
pneumonia	肺炎	**haien**
sprain	捻挫	**nenza**

EXERCISE
8·14

Complete each of the following sentences with the appropriate word.

1. 鼻水が _____ ます。

   Hanamizu ga _____ masu.

   I have a runny nose.

2. 熱が _____ ます。

   Netsu ga _____ masu.

   I have a fever.

3. _____ が出ます。

   _____ ga demasu.

   I cough.

4. 頭が _____ です。

   Atama ga _____ desu.

   I have a headache.

EXERCISE
8·15

Read the following dialog between a patient and a doctor and answer the questions that follow.

DOCTOR どうしましたか。

Dō shimashita ka.

What happened?

PATIENT 咳が出るんです。それに熱があります。

Seki ga deru n desu. Soreni netsu ga arimasu.

DOCTOR ああ, そうですか。

Ā, sō desu ka.

PATIENT それから頭が痛いです。

Sorekara atama ga itai desu.

DOCTOR 喉は。

Nodo wa?

PATIENT 喉は痛くありません。

Nodo wa itaku arimasen.

[The doctor checks the patient.]

DOCTOR 肺炎かもしれません。

Haien kamo shiremasen.

1. Does the patient have a fever? _____

2. Does he have a cough? _____

3. Does he have a sore throat? _____

4. What is the doctor's conclusion? _____

Listing and connecting actions and states by using the **te** form

You can list actions and states in one sentence by using the **te** form. The **te** form does not bear tense, so it cannot complete a sentence, but includes the meaning *and*, so it has to be followed by another instance of a verb or an adjective, which might bear tense. The last verb or adjective in the sentence should not be in the **te** form but should appear in the regular form, bearing a tense. Depending on the context, **te** forms can list temporally ordered actions, additional properties, and cause-effect relationships.

To form a **te** form of an adjective, add くて **kute** to the stem of an **i** adjectives or で **de** to the stem of a **na** adjective. The **te** form of the adjective いい **ii** is よくて **yokute**. To form the negative **te** forms, just replace くて **kute** or で **de** in their affirmative **te** forms with くなくて **ku nakute** or じゃなくて **ja nakute**.

Chapter 5 explains how to form a **te** form of a verb. The representative forms of all of the **te** forms are listed in the following table:

	AFFIRMATIVE	NEGATIVE
Verbs	食べて **tabete** *eat and*	食べなくて or 食べないで **tabenakute** or **tabenai de** *not eat and*
Noun + copula	犬で **inu de** *be a dog and*	犬じゃなくて **inu ja nakute** *be not a dog and*
Na adjective	高価で **kōka de** *be expensive and*	高価じゃなくて **kōka ja nakute** *be not expensive and*
I adjective	高くて **takakute** *be expensive and*	高くなくて **takaku nakute** *be not expensive and*

Verbs have two kinds of negative **te** forms: . . . なくて **nakute** and . . . ないで **naide**. Use . . . なくて **nakute** only if it creates a cause-effect relationship.

子供がご飯を食べなくて困っています。
Kodomo ga gohan o tabenakute komatte imasu.
My child does not eat meals and (so) I'm troubled.

朝ごはんを食べないでクラスに行きました。
Asa-gohan o tabenai de kurasu ni ikimashita.
I did not eat breakfast, and then I went to class. (I went to class without eating breakfast.)

EXERCISE
8·16

*Connect the words in each set by using the **te** form.*

1. 昨日 **kinō** *yesterday*, テレビを見る **terebi o miru** *to watch TV*, 宿題をする **shukudai o suru** *to do homework*, 寝る **neru** *to sleep*

   _____

   _____

2. あした **ashita** *tomorrow*, 掃除をする **sōji o suru** *to clean*, 買い物をする **kaimono o suru** *to go shopping*, 料理をする **ryōri o suru** *to cook*

   _____

   _____

3. マイクさん **Maiku-san** *Mike*, 頭がいい **atama ga ii** *to be smart*, 優しい **yasashii** *to be kind*, かっこいい **kakko ii** *to be good-looking*

   _____

   _____

4. メアリーさん **Mearī-san** *Mary*, きれいだ **kirei da** *to be pretty*, 頭がいい **atama ga ii** *to be smart*

   _____

   _____

5. このレストランのすし **kono resutoran no sushi** *this restaurant's sushi*, 高くない **takaku nai** *not to be expensive*, おいしい **oishii** *to be delicious*

   _____

   _____

For each of the following, choose the correct answer from the options in parentheses.

1. あまりきれい（じゃなくて, くなくて）よくありません。

   Amari kirei (ja nakute, ku nakute) yoku arimasen.

   It's not pretty, and it's not good.

2. シャワーを（あびないで, あびなくて）学校に行きました。

   Shawā o (abinai de, abinakute) gakkō ni ikimashita.

   I went to school without taking a shower.

3. 田中さんが（来ないで, 来なくて）困りました。

   Tanaka-san ga (konai de, konakute) komarimashita.

   Mr. Tanaka did not come, so I was in trouble.

4. ここでタバコを（すわないで, すわなくて）ください。

   Koko de tabako o (suwanai de, suwanakute) kudasai.

   Please do not smoke here.

5. 昨日は早く（おきられなくて, おきられないで）、クラスに遅れました。

   Kinō wa hayaku (okirarenakute, okirarenai de), kurasu ni okuremashita.

   I could not wake up early and was late for class.

   (. . . に遅れる **ni okureru** means *to be late for . . .*)

*Translate the following sentences into Japanese using **te** forms.*

1. *Please ask me and then buy (it).*

   (私に聞く **watashi ni kiku** means *to ask me*)

   _____

2. *Don't eat without washing your hands.*

   _____

3. *I took medicine because I had a headache.*

   (薬をのむ **kusuri o nomu** means *to take medicine*)

   _____

The clause conjunctions が ga and から kara

Here you'll learn about two conjunctions: が **ga** and から **kara**.

The conjunction が **ga**

To express two contrasting or conflicting events or states in the same sentence, use the conjunction particle が **ga**. For example:

高いですが買います。
Takai desu ga kaimasu.
It's expensive, but I'll buy it.

これは高いですがあれは安いです。
Kore wa takai desu ga are wa yasui desu.
This one is expensive, but that one is cheap.

Interestingly, が **ga** can also simply connect two sentences when there is a logical transition, even if there is no conflict or contrast. For example:

佐藤と申しますが社長にお会いできますか。
Satō to mōshimasu ga shachō ni o-ai dekimasu ka.
My name is Sato. Could I see the president of your company?

これは日本で買ったんですがとても便利ですよ。
Kore wa Nihon de katta n desu ga totemo benri desu yo.
I bought this in Japan and it is very convenient!

これは終わりましたが次は何をしましょうか。
Kore wa owarimashita ga tsugi wa nani o shimashō ka.
I finished this one. What shall I do next?

When you use が **ga**, make sure to use the same form for the predicate in the **ga** clause and the predicate in the main clause: both plain forms or both polite forms.

The conjunction から **kara**

The clause conjunction particle から **kara** can create a reason clause, as shown here:

高いですから売れません。
Takai desu kara uremasen.
It's expensive, so it does not sell well.

高いですから買わないでください。
Takai desu kara kawanai de kudasai.
Because it is expensive, please do not buy it.

It is better to use the same form for the predicate in the **kara** clause and the predicate in the main clause: both plain forms or both polite forms.

Combine each pair of sentences into a single sentence.

1. おいしくありませんでした。でも食べました。

   Oishiku arimasendeshita. Demo tabemashita.

   It was not delicious. However, I ate it.

   _____

2. 美香さんはきれいです。でも意地悪です。

   Mika-san wa kirei desu. Demo ijiwaru desu.

   Mika is pretty. However, she is mean.

   _____

3. 日本語の試験を受けたいんです。どう思いますか。

   Nihongo no shiken o uke-tai n desu. Dō omoimasu ka.

   I want to take a Japanese exam. What do you think?

   _____

4. 3級は難しいです。ですから4級を受けるつもりです。

   San-kyū wa muzukashii desu. Desu kara yon-kyū o ukeru tsumori desu.

   Level 3 is hard. Therefore, I plan to take Level 4.

   _____

5. 明日うちに田中さんが来ます。山田さんも来ませんか。

   Ashita uchi ni Tanaka-san ga kimasu. Yamada-san mo kimasen ka.

   Mr. Tanaka will come to my house tomorrow. Would you like to come, too, Ms. Yamada?

   _____

Review exercises

Chapter 1   Let's say and write Japanese words!

EXERCISE
9·1

Read the following words written in hiragana aloud. For a greater challenge, cover the romaji as you work on this exercise.

1.	あか	**aka**	*red*
2.	つき	**tsuki**	*the moon*
3.	さかな	**sakana**	*fish*
4.	おりがみ	**origami**	*origami*
5.	みなみ	**minami**	*south*
6.	てんぷら	**tenpura**	*tempura*
7.	こおり	**kōri**	*ice*
8.	おっと	**otto**	*one's husband*
9.	としょかん	**toshokan**	*library*

EXERCISE
9·2

Read the following words written in katakana aloud. For a greater challenge, cover the romaji as you work on this exercise.

1.	アニメ	**anime**	*anime*
2.	アメリカ	**Amerika**	*America*
3.	ロンドン	**Rondon**	*London*
4.	コーヒー	**kōhī**	*coffee*
5.	パソコン	**pasokon**	*computer, p.c.*
6.	ベッド	**beddo**	*bed*
7.	テニス	**tenisu**	*tennis*
8.	ホテル	**hoteru**	*hotel*
9.	バイオリン	**baiorin**	*violin*

Read the following Japanese words written in kanji aloud. For a greater challenge, cover the romaji as you work on this exercise.

1. 人   **hito**   *person*
2. 日本人   **Ni-hon-jin**   *a Japanese person*
3. 三人   **san-nin**   *three people*
4. 口   **kuchi**   *mouth*
5. 人口   **jin-kō**   *population*
6. 川   **kawa**   *river*
7. 川口   **kawa-guchi**   *Kawaguchi (a Japanese family name)*
8. 山   **yama**   *mountain*
9. 富士山   **Fu-ji-san**   *Mt. Fuji*

Read the following sentence written in mixed Japanese scripts aloud. For a greater challenge, cover the romaji as you work on this exercise.

エミリーは日本人です。

Emirī wa Nihon-jin desu.

Emily is Japanese.

Chapter 2   Getting to know someone

Reorder the items in each set to form a grammatical sentence and translate it.

1. {の **no**, 日本語 **Nihon-go**, です **desu**, 私 **watashi**, 学生 **gakusei**, は **wa**}

   _____

2. {私 **watashi**, 中国 **Chūgoku**, は **wa**, です **desu**, から **kara**}

   _____

3. {日本人 **Nihon-jin**, は **wa**, じゃありません **ja arimasen**, ケンさん **Ken-san**}

   _____

4. {人 hito, あの ano, です desu, は wa, か ka, だれ dare}

   _____

5. {人 hito, あの ano, 妹さん imōto-san, です desu, は wa, の no, 谷さん Tani-san}

   _____

EXERCISE 9·6

Find five country names in the puzzle, either vertically (top to bottom) or horizontally (left to right):

パ	ワ	エ	ク	コ	セ
リ	ボ	ス	ト	ン	イ
カ	シ	イ	ロ	ク	ロ
オ	ア	タ	ン	チ	ン
ナ	フ	ラ	ト	ス	ド
ロ	ー	マ	ド	イ	ン

EXERCISE 9·7

For each of the following, choose the correct answer from the options in parentheses:

1. 谷さんのお姉さんは（あれ, あの）人です。

   Tani-san no onēsan wa (are, ano) hito desu. *Mr. Tani's older sister is that person.*

2. （あの人, あれ）は山田さんです。

   (Ano hito, Are) wa Yamada-san desu. *That person is Ms. Yamada.*

3. （これ, この）車は日本の車です。

   (Kore, Kono) kuruma wa Nihon no kuruma desu. *This car is a Japanese car.*

4. （それ, あの）は何ですか。

   (Sore, Ano) wa nan desu ka. *What is that?*

5. （これ, この）は私の本です。

   (Kore, Kono) wa watashi no hon desu. *This is my book.*

EXERCISE

9·8

What would you say in Japanese in the following situations?

1. *You met someone for the first time. You are about to tell her your name.*

_____

2. *Your friend's mother served you a cup of coffee.*

_____

3. *Your accidentally stepped on someone else's foot in a bus.*

_____

4. *It's 9 AM. You see your Japanese teacher in front of the library.*

_____

Chapter 3 Using numbers

EXERCISE

9·9

Read the following number phrases aloud. Then, write them down in hiragana or romaji:

1. ３００ドル (300 dollars)　_____

2. １,０００円 (1,000 yen)　_____

3. ０３-６７４２-１５８３ (phone number) _____

4. ２３歳 (age)　_____

5. ７月２１日 (July 21st)　_____

6. 午後４時 (4 PM)　_____

7. 午前５時１５分 (5:15 AM)　_____

8. ２０１８年 (2018)　_____

9. ５つ (5 pieces)　_____

EXERCISE

9·10

Choose the correct English translation from the options in parentheses:

1. 水曜日　　　**Suiyōbi**　　　*(Monday, Wednesday, Friday)*

2. 火曜日　　　**Kayōbi**　　　*(Sunday, Tuesday, Friday)*

3. 金曜日　　　**Kinyōbi**　　　*(Sunday, Friday, Thursday)*

4. 土曜日   **Doyōbi**   (*Sunday, Thursday, Saturday*)

5. 月曜日   **Getsuyōbi**   (*Monday, Thursday, Saturday*)

EXERCISE
9·11

Answer the following questions in Japanese based on the fact. (Answers vary.)

1. 誕生日はいつですか。

   Tanjōbi wa itsu desu ka. *When is your birthday?*

   _____

2. あしたは何曜日ですか。

   Ashita wa nanyōbi desu ka. *What date is it tomorrow?*

   _____

3. 今, 何時ですか。

   Ima nan-ji desu ka. *What time is it now?*

   _____

4. 今, 何月ですか。

   Ima nan-gatsu desu ka. *What month is it now?*

   _____

EXERCISE
9·12

Translate the following sentences into Japanese:

1. *How much is that camera?* (*camera:* カメラ **kamera**)

   _____

2. *May I have this camera and that scanner?* (*scanner:* スキャナー **sukyanā**)

   _____

3. *Please give me three postage stamps.* (*postage stamp:* 切手 **kitte**)

   _____

4. There are two cats. (*cat:* ねこ **neko**)

   _____

5. There are three books. (*book:* 本 **hon**)

   _____

Chapter 4   Around town

Match the words in the two columns.

1. 飛行機 **hikōki** _____   *a. airplane*

2. バス **basu** _____   *b. subway*

3. 車 **kuruma** _____   *c. car*

4. 地下鉄 **chikatetsu** _____   *d. train*

5. 電車 **densha** _____   *e. bus*

Change the following verbs to their ***masu*** form. The verb class is specified only when it is not predictable based on the ending sound of the verb.

1. 行く **iku** (*go*)   _____

2. 来る **kuru** (*come*, irregular)   _____

3. 帰る **kaeru** (*return*, **u** verb)   _____

4. 歩く **aruku** (*walk*)   _____

5. 買う **kau** (*buy*)   _____

6. 待つ **matsu** (*wait*)   _____

7. 食べる **taberu** (*eat*, **ru** verb)   _____

8. 泳ぐ **oyogu** (*swim*)   _____

9. する **suru** (*do*, irregular)   _____

Translate the following sentences into Japanese.

1. *I will go to the supermarket today.* (supermarket: スーパー **sūpā**)

   _____

2. *I will not go anywhere tomorrow.*

   _____

3. *Will you go to somewhere tomorrow?*

_____

4. *Where will you go today?*

_____

EXERCISE
9·16

For each of the following, choose the correct answer from the options in parentheses.

1. 田中さんは車（に, で）大学に行きます。(車 **kuruma**: *car*)

   Tanaka-san wa kuruma (ni, de) daigaku ni ikimasu.

2. 土曜日は会社（に, で）行きません。(会社 **kaisha**: *company*)

   Doyōbi wa kaisha (ni, de) ikimasen.

3. よくレストランに（行きます, 行きません）。

   Yoku resutoran ni (ikimasu, ikimasen).

4. カラオケにはあまり（行きます, 行きません）。

   Karaoke ni wa amari (ikimasu, ikimasen).

5. 母は３時ぐらいに（帰ります, 帰りませんか）。(母 **haha**: *one's own mother*)

   Haha wa san-ji gura ni (kaerimasu, kaerimasen ka).

6. 映画を（見る, 見）に行きませんか。(映画 **eiga**: *movie*)

   Eiga o (miru, mi) ni ikimasenka.

7. 会社に（歩いて, 歩きます）行きます。(歩く **aruku**: *walk*)

   Kaisha ni (aruite, arukimasu) ikimasu.

Chapter 5   Talking about activities

EXERCISE
9·17

*Conjugate the following verbs into the **nai** form (plain non-past negative form). The verb class is specified only when it is not predictable based on the ending sound of the verb.*

1. うたう **utau** *sing*   _____ *not sing*

2. 作る **tsukuru** *make*   _____ *not make*

3. 切る **kiru** (**u** verb) *cut*   _____ *not cut*

4. 着る **kiru** (**ru** verb) *wear*   _____ *not wear*

5. 寝る **neru** (**ru** verb) *sleep* _____ *not sleep*

6. 起きる **okiru** (**ru** verb) *wake up* _____ *not wake up*

7. 来る **kuru** (irregular) *come* _____ *not come*

8. する **suru** (irregular) *do* _____ *not do*

EXERCISE
9·18

*Conjugate the following verbs into the **te** form.*

1. 買う **kau** *buy* _____ *buy and …*

2. 読む **yomu** *read* _____ *read and …*

3. 話す **hanasu** *speak* _____ *speak and …*

EXERCISE
9·19

Conjugate the following verbs into the potential form.

1. 書く **kaku** *write* _____ *be able to write*

2. 飛ぶ **tobu** *fly* _____ *be able to fly*

3. 泳ぐ **oyogu** *swim* _____ *be able to swim*

EXERCISE
9·20

For each of the following, choose the correct answer from the options in parentheses.

1. 見ました。(ですから, でも), 買いませんでした。

Mimashita. (Desukara, Demo), kaimasendeshita. *(I) saw (it). However, (I) didn't buy (it).*

2. 駐車場で森さん(を, に)見ました。

Chūshajō de Mori-san (o, ni) mimashita. *(I) saw Mr. Mori in the parking lot.*

3. 母 (が, を)てんぷらを作りました。

Haha (ga, o) tenpura o tsukurimashita. *My mother made tenpura.*

4. 兄はボストン(に, で)勉強しています。

Ani wa Bosuton (ni, de) benkyō-shite imasu. *My older brother is studying in Boston.*

5. フォークとナイフ（を, で）食べませんでした。

   Fōku to naifu (o, de) tabemasendeshita. *(I) didn't eat with fork and knife.*

6. 今晩は（ねません, ねない）つもりです。

   Konban wa (nemasen, nenai) tsumori desu. *I plan not to sleep tonight.*

7. 姉はフランス語が（はなし, はなせ）ます。

   Ane wa Furansu-go ga (hanashi, hanase) masu. *My older sister can speak French.*

8. タバコを（すわない, すわないで）ください。

   Tabako o (suwanai, suwanaide) kudasai. *Please do not smoke.*

9. 田中さんはまだ（来ませんでした, 来ていません）。

   Tanaka-san wa mada (kimasendeshita, kite imasen). *Mr. Tanaka has not come yet.*

10. お母さん（が, と）あそびに来てください。

    Okāsan (ga, to) asobi ni kite kudasai. *Please come to visit (us) with your mother.*

Chapter 6   Talking about people and things and their locations

EXERCISE 9·21

Match the words in the two columns.

1. 東 **higashi** _____   a. *front*

2. 西 **nishi** _____   b. *left*

3. 右 **migi** _____   c. *right*

4. 左 **hidari** _____   d. *east*

5. 前 **mae** _____   e. *west*

EXERCISE 9·22

Reorder the items in each set to form a grammatical sentence.

1. {あります **arimasu**, は **wa**, かばん **kaban**, の **no**, ペン **pen**, 中 **naka**, に **ni**}

   The pen is in the bag.

   _____

2. {あります **arimasu**, 名古屋は **Nagoya wa**, 間に **aida ni**, 大阪 **Ōsaka**, と **to**, 東京 **Tōkyō**, の **no**}

   Nagoya is between Tokyo and Osaka.

   _____

   _____

Fill in the blanks with います, あります, *or* いらっしゃいます.

1. あそこに桜の木が＿＿＿＿＿＿＿。

   Asoko ni sakura no ki ga ＿＿＿＿＿＿＿. *There is a cherry tree over there.*

2. あ！あそこに兎が＿＿＿＿＿＿よ。

   A! Asoko ni usagi ga ＿＿＿＿＿＿ yo. *Oh! There is a rabbit over there!*

3. あそこに森先生が＿＿＿＿＿＿ ね。

   Asoko ni Mori sensei ga ＿＿＿＿＿＿ ne. *Professor Mori is over there, isn't she?*

4. 母は兄弟が３人＿＿＿＿＿＿。

   Haha wa kyōdai ga san-nin ＿＿＿＿＿＿. *My mother has three siblings.*

5. うちには冷蔵庫が２台＿＿＿＿＿＿。

   Uchi ni wa reizōko ga ni-dai ＿＿＿＿＿＿. *We have two refrigerators in our house.*

6. うちの隣に花屋が ＿＿＿＿＿＿。

   Uchi no tonari ni hana-ya ga ＿＿＿＿＿＿. *There's a flower shop next to my house.*

7. あさっては試験が＿＿＿＿＿＿。

   Asatte wa shiken ga ＿＿＿＿＿＿. *I have an exam the day after tomorrow.*

8. 日本はよく地震が＿＿＿＿＿＿。

   Nihon wa yoku jishin ga ＿＿＿＿＿＿. *Japan is often hit by earthquakes.*

Choose the correct answer from the options in parentheses.

この道をまっすぐ行ってください。（1. それから, そうすると）, 7つ目の交差点を左に 曲がってください。（2. それから, そうすると）, 右に私の会社 があります。私の会社の前にはバス停があります。（3. ですから, でも）, バスでも行けますよ。

Kono michi o massugu itte kudasai. (1. Sorekara, Sōsuruto), nanatsu-me no kōsaten o hidari ni magatte kudasai. (2. Sorekara, Sōsuruto), migi ni watashi no kaisha ga arimasu. Watashi no kaisha no mae ni wa basu-tei ga arimasu. (3. Desukara, Demo), basu de mo ikemasu yo.

1. ＿＿＿＿＿＿＿＿   2. ＿＿＿＿＿＿＿＿   3. ＿＿＿＿＿＿＿＿

Chapter 7 Describing things

EXERCISE 9·25

Match the words and phrases that mean the opposite to each other.

1. 大きいです **ōkii desu** _____

2. 書きやすいです **kaki-yasui desu** _____

3. 簡単です **kantan desu** _____

4. おいしいです **oishii desu** _____

5. 好きです **suki desu** _____

6. 上手です **jōzu desu** _____

7. 大人っぽいです **otonappoi desu** _____

8. 背が低いです **se ga hikui desu** _____

a. 難しいです **muzukashii desu**

b. 背が高いです **se ga takai desu**

c. 子供っぽいです **kodomoppoi desu**

d. 下手です **heta desu**

e. 嫌いです **kirai desu**

f. まずいです **mazui desu**

g. 小さいです **chīsai desu**

h. 書きにくいです **kaki-nikui desu**

EXERCISE 9·26

In each of the following, choose the appropriate answer from the options in parentheses.

1. スカートを(着て, はいて)います。(スカート **skāto**: *skirt*)

   Sukāto o (kite, haite) imasu.

2. ネックレスを(して, かぶって)います。(ネックレス **Nekkuresu**: *necklace*)

   Nekkuresu o (shite, kabutte) imasu.

3. このパソコンはぜんぜん(高いです, 高くありません)。(パソコン **pasokon**: *pc*)

   Kono pasokon wa zenzen (takai desu, takaku arimasen).

4. カタカナはひらがな(と, より)同じぐらい簡単です。(簡単 **kantan**: *easy*)

   Katakana wa hiragana (to, yori) onaji gurai kantan desu.

5. 昨日の晩は(寒い, 寒かった)です。(寒い **samui**: *cold*)

   Kinō no ban wa (samui, samukatta) desu.

Complete each of the following sentences with an appropriate word or phrase:

1. 母は父＿＿＿＿＿きびしいです。

   Haha wa chichi ＿＿＿＿＿ kibishii desu. *My mother is stricter than my father.*

2. ルームメートは＿＿＿＿＿人ですか。

   Rūmumēto wa ＿＿＿＿＿ hito desu ka。 *What kind of person is your roommate?*

3. ＿＿＿＿＿冬が一番好きなんですか。

   ＿＿＿＿＿ fuyu ga ichiban suki na n desu ka. *Why do you like winter the best?*

4. 静かに＿＿＿＿＿ ください。

   Shizuka ni ＿＿＿＿＿ kudasai. *Please be quiet.*

5. 京都＿＿＿＿＿奈良に行きました。

   Kyōto ＿＿＿＿＿ Nara ni ikimashita. *I went to Kyoto, Nara, etc.*

EXERCISE
9·28

Translate the following sentences into Japanese:

1. *I like manga a lot. As a result, I read manga too much.* (*manga:* マンガ **manga**)

   _____

2. *I want to eat sushi. However, it is too expensive.*

   _____

3. *I tried this dress. However, I did not like it. In addition, it was too expensive.*

   _____

4. *I like cleaning. I made kitchen clean yesterday.* (*kitchen:* キッチン **kitchin**)

   _____

Chapter 8 Making connections

EXERCISE
9·29

Match the words in the two columns.

1. おなかが痛い **onaka ga itai** _____   a. *to have a fever*

2. 咳が出る **seki ga deru** _____   b. *to have nausea*

3. 熱がある **netsu ga aru** _____

c. *to have a stomachache*

4. 頭が痛い **atama ga itai** _____

d. *to have a headache*

5. 吐き気がする **hakike ga suru** _____

e. *to cough*

Match the words in the two columns.

1. 曇り **kumori** _____

a. *clear weather (sky)*

2. 雪 **yuki** _____

b. *cloudy weather (sky)*

3. 晴れ **hare** _____

c. *rain*

4. 台風 **taifū** _____

d. *snow*

5. 雨 **ame** _____

e. *typhoon*

Rephrase the following Japanese sentences using the item in the parentheses so that you can express the intended meaning specified in English.

1. 数学は簡単です。(…と思います)

   Sūgaku wa kantan desu. (… to omoimasu) *I think math is easy.*

   _____

2. 飲みすぎました。(…かもしれません)

   Nomi-sugimashita. (… kamoshiremasen) *I may have drunk too much.*

   _____

3. 日曜日は雪がふります。(…でしょう)

   Nichiyōbi wa yuki ga furimasu. (… deshō) *It will probably snow on Sunday.*

   _____

4. 富士山を見ましたか。(…ことがありますか)

   Fuji-san o mimashita ka. (… koto ga arimasu ka) *Have you ever seen Mt. Fuji?*

   _____

5. 来月結婚します。(…んです)

   Raigetsu kekkon shimasu. (… n desu) *It is the case that I'll get married next month.*

   _____

*Combine each pair of sentences into a single sentence using が **ga** or から **kara**.*

1. 高かったです。でも, よかったです。

   Takakatta desu. Demo, yokatta desu. *(It) was expensive. However, (it) was good.*

   _____

2. これは日本で買ったんです。とても便利ですよ。

   Kore wa Nihon de katta n desu. Totemo benri desu yo.

   (I) bought this in Japan. It is very convenient!

   _____

3. 朝ごはんを食べないでクラスに行きました。ですから今おなかがすいています。

   Asa-gohan o tabenai de kurasu ni ikimashita. Desukara ima onaka ga suite imasu.

   I went to class without eating breakfast. So I am hungry.

   _____

Appendix 1

The stations on the Yamanote Line in Tokyo

山手線

Yamanotesen

Yamanote Line in Tokyo

1	東京 Tōkyō		16	新大久保 Shin-Okubo
2	神田 Kanda		17	新宿 Shinjuku
3	秋葉原 Akihabara		18	代々木 Yoyogi
4	御徒町 Okachimachi		19	原宿 Harajuku
5	上野 Ueno		20	渋谷 Shibuya
6	鶯谷 Uguisudani		21	恵比寿 Ebisu
7	日暮里 Nippori		22	目黒 Meguro
8	西日暮里 Nishi-Nippori		23	五反田 Gotanda
9	田端 Tabata		24	大崎 Ōsaki
10	駒込 Komagome		25	品川 Shinagawa
11	巣鴨 Sugamo		26	高輪ゲートウエイ Takanawa Gateway
12	大塚 Ōtsuka		27	田町 Tamachi
13	池袋 Ikebukuro		28	浜松町 Hamamatsuchō
14	目白 Mejiro		29	新橋 Shinbashi
15	高田馬場 Takadanobaba		30	有楽町 Yūrakuchō

Appendix 2
Prefectures in Japan

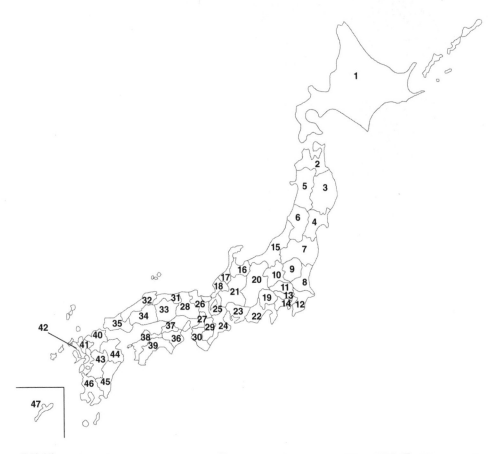

1.	北海道 Hokkaidō	17.	石川県 Ishikawa-ken	33.	岡山県 Okayama-ken
2.	青森県 Aomori-ken	18.	福井県 Fukui-ken	34.	広島県 Hiroshima-ken
3.	岩手県 Iwate-ken	19.	山梨県 Yamanashi-ken	35.	山口県 Yamaguchi-ken
4.	宮城県 Miyagi-ken	20.	長野県 Nagano-ken	36.	徳島県 Tokushima-ken
5.	秋田県 Akita-ken	21.	岐阜県 Gifu-ken	37.	香川県 Kagawa-ken
6.	山形県 Yamagata-ken	22.	静岡県 Shizuoka-ken	38.	愛媛県 Ehime-ken
7.	福島県 Fukushima-ken	23.	愛知県 Aichi-ken	39.	高知県 Kōchi-ken
8.	茨城県 Ibaraki-ken	24.	三重県 Mie-ken	40.	福岡県 Fukuoka-ken
9.	栃木県 Tochigi-ken	25.	滋賀県 Shiga-ken	41.	佐賀県 Saga-ken
10.	群馬県 Gunma-ken	26.	京都府 Kyōto-fu	42.	長崎県 Nagasaki-ken
11.	埼玉県 Saitama-ken	27.	大阪府 Ōsaka-fu	43.	熊本県 Kumamoto-ken
12.	千葉県 Chiba-ken	28.	兵庫県 Hyōgo-ken	44.	大分県 Ōita-ken
13.	東京都 Tōkyō-to	29.	奈良県 Nara-ken	45.	宮崎県 Miyazaki-ken
14.	神奈川県 Kanagawa-ken	30.	和歌山県 Wakayama-ken	46.	鹿児島県 Kagoshima-ken
15.	新潟県 Nīgata-ken	31.	鳥取県 Tottori-ken	47.	沖縄県 Okinawa-ken
16.	富山県 Toyama-ken	32.	島根県 Shimane-ken		

Appendix 3

Some commonly used verb forms

	Dictionary form	Nai form	Ta form	Nakatta form	Stem form	Te form
Ru verbs	ねる **neru** "sleep"	ねない **nenai**	ねた **neta**	ねなかった **nenakatta**	ね **ne**	ねて **nete**
	みる **miru** "look"	みない **minai**	みた **mita**	みなかった **minakatta**	み **mi**	みて **mite**
U verbs	とる **toru** "take"	とらない **toranai**	とった **totta**	とらなかった **toranakatta**	とり **tori**	とって **totte**
	かく **kaku** "write"	かかない **kakanai**	かいた **kaita**	かかなかった **kakanakatta**	かき **kaki**	かいて **kaite**
	およぐ **oyogu** "swim"	およがない **oyoganai**	およいだ **oyoida**	およがなかった **oyoganakatta**	およぎ **oyogi**	およいで **oyoide**
	おす **osu** "push"	おさない **osanai**	おした **oshita**	おさなかった **osanakatta**	おし **oshi**	おして **oshite**
	かう **kau** "buy"	かわない **kawanai**	かった **katta**	かわなかった **kawanakatta**	かい **kai**	かって **katte**
	かつ **katsu** "win"	かたない **katanai**	かった **katta**	かたなかった **katanakatta**	かち **kachi**	かって **katte**
	よむ **yomu** "read"	よまない **yomanai**	よんだ **yonda**	よまなかった **yomanakatta**	よみ **yomi**	よんで **yonde**
	しぬ **shinu** "die"	しなない **shinanai**	しんだ **shinda**	しななかった **shinanakatta**	しに **shini**	しんで **shinde**
	とぶ **tobu** "fly"	とばない **tobanai**	とんだ **tonda**	とばなかった **tobanakatta**	とび **tobi**	とんで **tonde**
Irregular verbs	する **suru** "do"	しない **shinai**	した **shita**	しなかった **shinakatta**	し **shi**	して **shite**
	くる **kuru** "come"	こない **konai**	きた **kita**	こなかった **konakatta**	き **ki**	きて **kite**

Dictionary form:	Plain affirmative non-past form
Nai form:	Plain negative non-past form
Ta form:	Plain affirmative past form
Nakatta form:	Plain negative past form
Stem form:	The stem form can be immediately followed by ますmasu, ません masen, ました mashita, ませんでした masendeshita, たい tai, やすい yasui, にくい nikui, and すぎる sugiru discussed in this book and some other items.
Te form:	It means "do ... and," and is used to list multiple verbs. It is also used to request someone do some action when immediately followed by ください kudasai.

Answer key

Answers are not given for oral or handwriting exercises or those that explore personal circumstances.

1   Let's say and write Japanese words!

1·5   1. かい   2. いけ   3. おか   4. あき   5. あお

1·9   1. つち   2. うち   3. て   4. たか   5. ちか   6. てつ

1·13   1. はし   2. くに   3. なし   4. あな   5. はか

1·16   1. *eye*   2. *ear*   3. *mouth*   4. *nose*   5. *foot*   6. *head*

1·17   1. c   2. b   3. d   4. a

1·18   1. くち   2. あたま   3. やま   4. かわ   5. ほし

1·20   1. おとうさん   2. おかあさん   3. おにいさん   4. おねえさん

1·22   1. しょどう   2. おりがみ   3. じゅうどう   4. きもの   5. いけばな

1·23   1. *Tokyo*   2. *Kyoto*   3. *Osaka*

1·24   1. ノ, フ, ヘ, レ   2. エキテニモ   3. ウ, カ, キ, セ, ヘ, モ, ヤ, ラ, リ, for example

1·25   1. シ **shi** and ツ **tsu**   2. ン **n** and ソ **so**   3. ク **ku** and ケ **ke**   4. ク **ku** and ワ **wa**   5. ク **ku** and タ **ta**   6. ロ **ro** and コ **ko**   7. ル **ru** and レ **re**   8. チ **chi** and テ **te**

1·26   1. *test*   2. *camera*   3. *necktie*   4. *hotel*

1·31   1. アメリカ   2. カナダ   3. ロシア   4. フランス

1·34   1. *mouth*   2. *mountain*   3. *river*   4. *fire*   5. *moon*   6. *tree*

2   Getting to know someone

2·1   こちらこそ **Kochira koso**

2·2   どちら **dochira**

2·3   1. e   2. d   3. c   4. b   5. a

2·4
1. イタリア **Italia** *Italy*
2. スペイン **Supein** *Spain*
3. ロシア **Roshia** *Russia*
4. インド **Indo** *India*
5. ドイツ **Doitsu** *Germany*
6. フランス **Furansu** *France*
7. タイ **Tai** *Thailand*
8. ケニア **Kenia** *Kenya*
9. チリ **Chiri** *Chile*

2·5
1. メイリンさんは北京からです。**Meirin-san wa Pekin kara desu.**
2. 由美子さんは東京からです。**Yumiko-san wa Tōkyō kara desu.**
3. トーマスさんはカナダからです。**Tōmasu-san wa Kanada kara desu.**
4. エミリーさんはイギリスからです。**Emirī-san wa igirisu kara desu.**

2·7
1. イタリア人 **Itaria-jin**   3. フィリピン人 **Firipin-jin**
2. カナダ人 **Kanada-jin**   4. インド人 **Indo-jin**

2·8
1. 武さんは日本人です。**Takeshi-san wa Nihon-jin desu.**
2. ヒージョンさんは韓国人です。**Hījon-san wa kankoku-jin desu.**
3. ブラウン先生はカナダ人です。**Buraun sensei wa Kanada-jin desu.**
4. チェンさんは中国人です。**Chen-san wa Chūgoku-jin desu.**
5. メイリンさんも中国人です。**Meirin-san mo Chūgoku-jin desu.**
6. ジョージさんはアメリカ人じゃありません。**Jōji-san wa Amerika-jin ja arimasen.** (or ジョージさんは アメリカ人じゃないです。**Jōji-san wa Amerika-jin ja nai desu.**)

2·10
1. あの女の人は日本人です。**Ano onna no hito wa Nihon-jin desu.**
2. あの男の人は中国人です。**Ano otoko no hito wa Chūgoku-jin desu.**
3. あの人は韓国人です。**Ano hito wa Kankoku-jin desu.**
4. あの子どもはフランス人です。**Ano kodomo wa Furansu-jin desu.**

2·11
1. 森さんは弁護士です。**Mori-san wa bengoshi desu.**
2. あの人は日本語の学生です。**Ano hito wa Nihon-go no gakusei desu.**
3. あの人は日本人の学生です。**Ano hito wa Nihon-jin no gakusei desu.**
4. あの女の人は先生です。**Ano onna no hito wa sensei desu.**
5. あの女の人は日本語の先生です。**Ano onna no hito wa Nihon-go no sensei desu.**

2·12
1. *Mr. Brown is a Japanese language teacher at a high school.*
2. *Mr. Tanaka works at an automobile factory.*
3. *Mike is a sales representative at a department store.*

2·13
1. 石田さんは大学の学生です。**Ishida-san wa daigaku no gakusei desu.** (or 石田さんは大学生です。 **Ishida-san wa daigakusei desu.**)
2. 谷さんは病院で働いています。**Tani-san wa byōin de hataraite imasu.**
3. 上田さんは日本の高校の英語の先生です。**Ueda-san wa Nihon no kōkō no eigo no sensei desu.**

2·14
1. Chinese
2. Japanese
3. works for a bank in Tokyo
4. teaches English in a high school in Yokohama
5. studies economics in a college in the United States

2·15
1. お姉さん **onēsan**
2. 父 **chichi**
3. 日本人 **Nihon-jin**
4. 日本語の学生 **Nihon-go no gakusei**
5. ケン **Ken**

2·16
1. 私は学生です。**Watashi wa gakusei desu.** *I am a student.*
2. 母は看護師です。**Haha wa kangoshi desu.** *My mother is a nurse.*
3. チェンさんは中国人じゃありません。**Chen-san wa Chūgoku-jin ja arimasen.** *Mr. Chen is not Chinese.*
4. チェンさんのお母さんは韓国人です。**Chen-san no okāsan wa Kankoku-jin desu.** *Mr. Chen's mother is Korean.*
5. あの人はだれですか。**Ano hito wa dare desu ka.** *Who is that person over there?*
6. あの人は山田さんの妹さんです。**Ano hito wa Yamada-san no imōtosan desu.** *That person is Ms. Yamada's younger sister.* or 山田さんの妹さんはあの人です。**Yamada-san no imōto-san wa ano hito desu.** *Ms. Yamada's younger sister is that person over there.*

2·17   1. True   2. False   3. True   4. False

2·19   はい **Hai**, ありません **arimasen**

2·20
1. 先生。おはようございます。**Sensei. Ohayō gozaimasu.**
2. おかあさん。おはよう。**Okāsan. Ohayō.**
3. いってきます。**Itte kimasu.**
4. じゃあ、しつれいします。さようなら。**Jā, shitsurei shimasu. Sayōnara.**

2·21   おはようございます **ohayō gozaimasu**, しつれい **Shitsurei**

2·22
1. あ、すみません。 A, sumimasen.
2. どうもありがとうございます。 Dōmo arigatō gozaimasu.
3. どうもすみません。 Dōmo sumimasen.
4. いいえ。 Īe.
5. いいえ。 Īe.

2·23 いいえ Īe

2·24 はい Hai

2·25 1. あれ Are   2. この Kono   3. それ sore   4. あの人 Ano hito

2·26 1. *key*   2. *wallet*   3. *sunglasses*   4. *computer*

2·27
1. A. *Whose umbrella is this?* B. *That's Ken's umbrella.*
2. A. *Whose is that?* B. *That's Jane's.*
3. A. *Whose car is that car?* B. *That's Mr. Tanaka's.*
4. A. *Which one is Mr. Smith's?* B. *That one.*
5. A. *What is that car?* B. *That's Toyota's Corolla.*

2·28
1. この Kono
2. それ sore
3. これ Kore
4. だれ dare
5. 何 nan
6. 山田さんの Yamada-san no (It's rude to refer to a person by using a demonstrative pronoun.)

2·29
1. あれは父の本です。 Are wa chichi no hon desu.
2. これは私のです。 Kore wa watashi no desu.
3. あの学生はだれですか。 Ano gakusei wa dare desu ka.
4. それは何ですか。 Sore wa nan desu ka.
5. ケンさんのはどれですか。 Ken-san no wa dore desu ka.

2·30 どれ dore, これ Kore

3   Using numbers

3·5
1. じゅうご jū-go
2. さんじゅうはち san-jū-hachi
3. ごじゅうろく go-jū-roku
4. ななじゅうなな nana-jū-nana
5. はちじゅうきゅう hachi-jū-kyū

3·6
1. にまん にせん にひゃく にじゅう に
   ni-man ni-sen ni-hyaku ni-jū-ni
2. さんまん さんぜん さんびゃく さんじゅうさん
   san-man san-zen san-byaku san-jū-san
3. ろくまんろくせんろっぴゃくろくじゅうろく
   roku-man roku-sen rop-pyaku roku-jū-roku
4. はちまんはっせんはっぴゃくはちじゅうはち
   Hachi-man has-sen hap-pyaku hachi-jū-hachi
5. きゅうまんきゅうせんきゅうひゃくきゅうじゅうきゅう
   kyū-man kyū-sen kyū-hyaku kyū-jū-kyū

3·7
1. いちまんきゅうせんはっぴゃく
   ichi-man kyū-sen hap-pyaku
2. よんまんよんせんななひゃくななじゅういち
   yon-man yon-sen nana-hyaku nana-jū-ichi
3. ごまんろくせんごひゃくにじゅうご
   go-man roku-sen go-hyaku ni-jū-go

3·14
1. *I don't know.* (ちょっと chotto is added to make the expression soft.)
2. *Then it's okay.* (or *Never mind.*)

3·15 1. 何時 nan-ji   2. どうも dōmo

3·16	1. 何時 **nan-ji**	2. 8時 **hachi-ji**

3·17
1. 午前6時35分 **Gozen roku-ji san-jū-go-fun**
2. 午後1時 **Gogo ichi-ji**

3·18
1. 月曜日 **Getsuyōbi**
2. 4月1日 **Shi-gatsu tsuitachi**
3. 午後9時 **gogo ku-ji**
4. 午前2時30分 **gozen ni-ji san-jup-pun** (or **gozen ni-ji han**)
5. 1998年 **sen-kyū-hyaku-kyū-jū-hachi-nen**

3·19 5月5日 **Go-gatsu itsuka**   2月14日 **Ni-gatsu jū-yok-ka**

3·22 1. いくら **ikura**   2. ください **kudasai**

3·23
1. ふたり **futa-ri** (2人)	4. ごさつ **go-satsu** (5冊)
2. にだい **ni-dai** (2台)	5. さんびき **san-biki** (3匹)
3. ふたつ **futa-tsu** (2つ)	6. いっぴき **ip-piki** (1匹)

3·24
1. 犬が2匹います。**Inu ga ni-hiki imasu.**
2. 切手が2枚あります。**Kitte ga ni-mai arimasu.**
3. 車が3台あります。**Kuruma ga san-dai arimasu.**
4. ノートを3冊ください。**Nōto o san-satsu kudasai.**
5. バナナを2本ください。**Banana o ni-hon kudasai.**
6. バナナを2本とりんごを3つください。**Banana o ni-hon to ringo o mit-tsu kudasai.**

4   Around town

4·1
1. 取ります **torimasu**	7. 買います **kaimasu**
2. 売ります **urimasu**	8. 書きます **kakimasu**
3. 始まります **hajimarimasu**	9. 泳ぎます **oyogimasu**
4. 作ります **tsukurimasu**	10. 運びます **hakobimasu**
5. 読みます **yomimasu**	11. 待ちます **machimasu**
6. 飲みます **nomimasu**	12. 話します **hanashimasu**

4·2
1. 変えます **kaemasu**	3. 食べます **tabemasu**
2. 着ます **kimasu**	4. 寝ます **nemasu**

4·3
1. 帰ります **kaerimasu**	3. 走ります **hashirimasu**
2. 切ります **kirimasu**	4. しゃべります **shaberimasu**

4·4
1. 作る **tsukuru**, 作ります **tsukurimasu**
2. 読む **yomu**, 読みます **yomimasu**
3. 書く **kaku**, 書きます **kakimasu**
4. 飲む **nomu**, 飲みます **nomimasu**
5. 行く **iku**, 行きます **ikimasu**
6. 勉強する **benkyō-suru**, 勉強します **benkyō-shimasu**
7. 来る **kuru**, 来ます **kimasu**

4·5
1. 食べます **tabemasu**
2. 帰ります **kaerimasu**
3. 寝ます **nemasu**

4·6
1. なります **narimasu**	9. 洗います **araimasu**
2. 売ります **urimasu**	10. 待ちます **machimasu**
3. 取ります **torimasu**	11. 持ちます **mochimasu**
4. 聞きます **kikimasu**	12. 休みます **yasumimasu**
5. 歩きます **arukimasu**	13. 住みます **sumimasu**
6. 貸します **kashimasu**	14. 死にます **shinimasu**
7. 話します **hanashimasu**	15. 選びます **erabimasu**
8. 会います **aimasu**	16. 運びます **hakobimasu**

4·7 1. **u** verb   2. **u** verb   3. **ru** verb   4. **ru** verb   5. **ru** verb   6. **ru** verb   7. **u** verb   8. **ru** verb
9. **ru** verb   10. **ru** verb

4·8 1. e   2. f   3. a   4. d   5. g   6. h   7. b   8. c

4·9
1. 行きません **ikimasen**	3. 行きます **ikimasu**
2. 来ます **kimasu**	4. 帰りますか **kaerimasu ka**

4·10
1. どこに **doko ni**
2. どこかに **dokoka ni**
3. どこにも行きません **doko ni mo ikimasen**

4·11
1. 今日は本屋に行きます。**Kyō wa hon'ya ni ikimasu.**
2. あしたはどこにも行きません。**Ashita wa doko ni mo ikimasen.**
3. あしたはどこかに行きますか。**Ashita wa dokoka ni ikimasu ka.**
4. 今日はどこに行きますか。**Kyō wa doko ni ikimasu ka.**

4·12
1. *I often go to restaurants.*
2. *I sometimes go to a department store.*
3. *I go to a park once in a while.*
4. *I don't go to a library very often.*
5. *I never go to karaoke.*

4·13
1. 行きます **ikimasu**   2. 行きません **ikimasen**   3. 行きます **ikimasu**

4·14
1. *Why don't we go to see a movie tonight?*
2. *Why don't we go for camping?*
3. *Why don't we go shopping on Saturday?*
4. *Why don't we go to buy a Japanese dictionary tomorrow?*
5. *Why don't we visit (go for fun) Okinawa next year?*
6. *Why don't we visit Mike's home next week?*
7. *Around what time shall we go?*

4·15
1. 今日はスーパーに行きますか。**Kyō wa sūpā ni ikimasu ka.**
2. あしたはどこかに行きますか。**Ashita wa dokoka ni ikimasu ka.**
3. 来年日本に行きませんか。**Rainen Nihon ni ikimasen ka.**
4. レストランにはよく行きますか。**Resutoran ni wa yoku ikimasu ka.**
5. 図書館にはあまり行きません。**Toshokan ni wa amari ikimasen.**
6. 公園に行きましょう。**Kōen ni ikimashō.**

4·16
1. 車で **kuruma de**
2. バスと電車で **basu to densha de**
3. 歩いて **aruite**
4. タクシーで **takushī de**
5. 自転車で **jitensha de**

4·17
1. 45 minutes   2. 25 minutes   3. bus and subway

4·18
1. tonight, around 7 PM
2. Takeshi, George, Takako, and Yukiko
3. *It's great, indeed, right?*
4. *Certainly fine!*

5   Talking about activities

5·1
1. *I will read a magazine.*
2. *I will write a letter.*
3. *I will watch a movie.*
4. *I will play a game.*
5. *I will play the piano.*

5·2
1. に **ni**   2. を **o**   3. を **o**   4. を **o**   5. を **o**   6. を **o**   7. を **o**   8. に **ni**

5·3
1. に **ni**   2. で **de**   3. で **de**, に **ni**   4. に **ni**   5. で **de**   6. で **de**   7. で **de**, で **de**

5·4
1. で **de**, を **o**   2. を **o**, で **de**   3. で **de**, に **ni**   4. で **de**   5. で **de**   6. を **o**

5·5
On weekends, I usually go shopping in the morning. I often go to a department store. Then I eat at a restaurant. Then I watch a movie at a movie theater.

5·7
1. を **o**   2. が **ga**   3. が **ga**, を **o**, が **ga**   4. を **o**

5·8
1. を **o**   2. と **to**   3. と **to**   4. と **to**, を **o**   5. と **to**, を **o**

5·9
1. Mika's mother
2. breakfast on weekends
3. Sunday lunch

5·10
1. 食べました **tabemashita**
2. 食べません **tabemasen**
3. 話します **hanashimasu**
4. 話しません **hanashimasen**
5. しませんでした **shimasendeshita**

5·11
1. 飲まない **nomanai**
2. うたわない **utawanai**
3. 見ない **minai**
4. 走らない **hashiranai**
5. 作らない **tsukuranai**
6. 来ない **konai**
7. しない **shinai**
8. 行かない **ikanai**
9. 泳がない **oyoganai**
10. 遊ばない **asobanai**
11. 待たない **matanai**
12. 話さない **hanasanai**

5·12
1. 来年日本に行くつもりです。**Rainen Nihon ni iku tsumori desu.**
2. 大学院には行かないつもりです。**Daigakuin ni wa ikanai tsumori desu.**
3. 日曜日に掃除と洗濯と買い物をするつもりです。**Nichiyōbi ni sōji to sentaku to kaimono o suru tsumori desu.**
4. 今晩は寝ないつもりです。**Konban wa nenai tsumori desu.**

5·13
1. カタカナが書ける **katakana ga kakeru**
2. カタカナで名前が書ける **katakana de namae ga kakeru**
3. 漢字が読める **kanji ga yomeru**
4. 日本語が話せる **Nihon-go ga hanaseru**
5. 日本語で話せる **NIhon-go de hanaseru**
6. てんぷらが作れる **tenpura ga tsukureru**
7. 車が運転できる **kuruma ga unten dekiru**

5·15
1. かいて **kaite**
2. かって **katte**
3. いって **itte**
4. いって **itte**
5. かって **katte**
6. とんで **tonde**
7. よんで **yonde**
8. およいで **oyoide**
9. して **shite**
10. きて **kite**

5·16
1. 入ってください。**Haitte kudasai.**
2. 座ってください。**Suwatte kudasai.**
3. 休んでください。**Yasunde kudasai.**
4. この手紙を読んでください。**Kono tegami o yonde kudasai.**
5. また来てください。**Mata kite kudasai.**
6. タバコをすわないでください。**Tabako o suwanai de kudasai.**
7. しゃべらないでください。**Shaberanai de kudasai.**
8. 静かにしてください。**Shizuka ni shite kudasai.**

5·17
1. *My younger sister is watching TV now.*
2. *My older brother swims for one hour every morning.*
3. *Mr. Tanaka has not come yet.*
4. *My father has gone to Osaka.*
5. *My older sister is already married.*
6. *My younger brother has been playing a game since this morning continuously.*

5·19
1. She runs, plays tennis, and practices karate.
2. He cooks.
3. Takako is going to Ken's house .

6 Talking about people and things and their locations

6·1   1. d   2. e   3. a   4. c   5. b
6·2   1. b   2. c   3. d   4. a   5. f   6. e
6·3
1. あります **arimasu**
2. います **imasu**
3. います **imasu**
4. いらっしゃいます **irasshaimasu**
5. あります **arimasu**

6·4
1. 富士山はどこにありますか。**Fujisan wa doko ni arimasu ka.**
2. 山田さんのうちには犬がいます。**Yamada-san no uchi ni wa inu ga imasu.**
3. 田中さんはどこにいますか。**Tanaka-san wa doko ni imasu ka.**
4. 田中さんは図書館にいます。**Tanaka-san wa toshokan ni imasu.**
5. あそこにメアリーさんがいますよ。**Asoko ni Mearī-san ga imasu yo.**

6·5
1. テレビ **terebi**　2. 冷蔵庫 **reizōko**　3. ベッド **beddo**　4. 椅子 **isu**　5. 机 **tsukue**

6·7
1. マイクさんのうちにはテレビが3台あります。**Maiku-san no uchi ni wa terebi ga san-dai arimasu.**
2. 森さんのうちには庭がありません。**Mori-san no uchi ni wa niwa ga arimasen.**
3. メアリーさんのうちには地下室があります。**Mearī-san no uchi ni wa chikashitsu ga arimasu.**
4. ジョージさんのアパートには洗濯機と乾燥機がありません。**Jōji-san no apāto ni wa sentakuki to kansōki ga arimasen.**

6·8
1. three　2. one　3. five

6·10
1. 本箱は机の横にあります。**Honbako wa tsukue no yoko ni arimasu.**
2. 机は窓の前にあります。**Tsukue wa mado no mae ni arimasu.**
3. 辞書は机の引き出しの中にあります。**Jisho wa tsukue no hikidashi no naka ni arimasu.**
4. ソファーは机とベッドの間にあります。**Sofā wa tsukue to beddo no aida ni arimasu.**

6·11
1. 郵便局は大学の南にあります。**Yūbinkyoku wa daigaku no minami ni arimasu.**
2. レストランは病院と本屋の間にあります。**Resutoran wa byōin to hon'ya no aida ni arimasu.**
3. 銀行は市役所の隣にあります。**Ginkō wa shiyakusho no tonari ni arimasu.**
4. 私のアパートは小学校の近くにあります。**Watashi no apāto wa shōgakkō no chikaku ni arimasu.**

6·12
1. in the center of the town
2. on Sakura Street
3. five minutes by bicycle

6·13
1. この通りをまっすぐ行ってください。**Kono tōri o massugu itte kudasai.**
2. あの交差点を左に曲がってください。**Ano kōsaten o hidari ni magatte kudasai.**
3. バス停を過ぎてください。**Basu-tē o sugite kudasai.**
4. あの橋を渡ってください。**Ano hashi o watatte kudasai.**
5. 三つ目の角を右に曲がってください。**Mit-tsu-me no kado o migi ni magatte kudasai.**

6·14
の **no**, に **ni**, を **o**, が **ga**

6·15
1. *I have two younger sisters.*
2. *I have two younger sisters and one younger brother.*
3. *Do you have siblings, Ms. Yamada?* (or *Does Ms. Yamada have siblings?*)
4. *I don't have siblings.*
5. *My older brother has a fiancé.*
6. *Mr. Chen has 30 cousins.*

6·16
1. none　2. only child　3. one　4. three

6·17
1. *I have three classes today. So I will not go to work.*
2. *I have no job today. So why don't we go shopping together?*
3. *I have an interview and an exam tomorrow. So I cannot go anywhere today.*

6·18
1. Mondays, Wednesdays, and Fridays
2. Fridays
3. from 5 PM to 10 PM

6·20
1. March 11, 2011
2. Pacific Ocean's open sea, near Tohoku Region
3. a huge tsunami, fires, and a nuclear power plant accident

7　Describing things

7·1
1. 新しいです。**Atarashii desu.** (*It's new.*)
2. きれいです。**Kirei desu.** (*She is pretty.*)
3. にぎやかです。**Nigiyaka desu.** (*It's crowded and lively.*)
4. 難しいです。**Muzukashii desu.** (*It's difficult.*)
5. おいしいです。**Oishii desu.** (*It's delicious.*)

7·2
1. 古いです **furui desu**　2. 汚いです **kitanai desu**　3. 高いです **takai desu**　4. 明るいです **akarui desu**　5. 大きいです **ōkii desu**

7·3   1. いいえ, 新しくありません。Ie, atarashiku arimasen. (or いいえ, 新しくないです。Ie, atarashiku nai desu.) *No, it is not new.*
2. いいえ, 静かじゃありません。Ie, shizuka ja arimasen. (or いいえ, 静かじゃないです。Ie, shizuka ja nai desu.) *No, it is not quiet.*
3. いいえ, 広くありません。Ie, hiroku arimasen. (or いいえ, 広くないです。Ie, hiroku nai desu.) *No, it is not spacious.*

7·4   きれい Kirei

7·5   1. どんな donna   2. どう dō   3. どんな Donna

7·6   1. いいえ, 親切じゃありません。Ie, shinsetsu ja arimasen. (or いいえ, 親切じゃないです。Ie, shinsetsu ja nai desu.)
2. いいえ, 優しくありません。Ie, yasashiku arimasen. (or いいえ, 優しくないです。Ie, yasashiku nai desu.)
3. いいえ, まじめじゃありません。Ie, majime ja arimasen. (or いいえ, まじめじゃないです。Ie, majime ja nai desu.)
4. いいえ, 静かじゃありません。Ie, shizuka ja arimasen. (or いいえ, 静かじゃないです。Ie, shizuka ja nai desu.)

7·7   1. まあまあ māmā   2. ぜんぜん zenzen   3. ちょっと chotto   4. とても totemo

7·9   1. 背が高い se ga takai
2. やせています yasete imasu
3. 髪が短いです kami ga mijikai desu
4. 背が低いです se ga hikui desu

7·11   どんな donna, やさしい yasashii, まあまあ māmā

7·12   1. Yes   2. No   3. Chinese

7·14   1. Hokkaido has delicious food, hot springs, and ski areas. It is cool in summer and cold in winter. There is a famous Snow Festival in Sapporo.
2. Yes.
3. Kyoto has old temples and shrines.

7·16   1. おいしかったです oishikatta desu *was delicious*
2. まずかったです mazukatta desu *was bad taste*
3. 甘かったです amakatta desu *was sweet*
4. 塩辛かったです shiokarakatta desu *was salty*
5. 香りがよかったです kaori ga yokatta desu *had nice aromas*

7·17   1. おいしくありませんでした oishiku arimasendeshita (or おいしくなかったです oishiku nakattadesu) *was not delicious*
2. まずくありませんでした mazuku arimasendeshita (or まずくなかったです mazuku nakattadesu) *was not bad taste*
3. すっぱくありませんでした suppaku arimasendeshita (or すっぱくなかったです suppaku nakattadesu) *was not sour*
4. 苦くありませんでした nigaku arimasendeshita (or 苦くなかったです nigaku nakattadesu) *was not bitter*
5. 辛くありませんでした karaku arimasendeshita (or 辛くなかったです karaku nakattadesu) *was not spicy*

7·18   1. かったです katta desu
2. 高くありませんでした takaku arimasendeshita (or 高くなかったです takaku nakatta desu)
3. よかったです yokatta desu

7·19   1. *I hate vegetables. However, my older sister loves vegetables.*
2. *Ms. Yamada is good at playing the piano.*
3. *My older brother is not good at talking with people.*
4. *My older sister is good at playing tennis. She plays tennis with her friend every morning.*

7·21   1. car and smartphone   2. in his friend's car   3. McDonald's restaurant

7·23   1. 着て kite   2. はいて haite   3. かぶって kabutte   4. して shite

7·24   1. このコートは長すぎます。Kono kōto wa naga-sugimasu.
2. このドレスは地味すぎます。Kono doresu wa jimi-sugimasu.
3. このネックレスは高すぎます。Kono nekkuresu wa taka-sugimasu.

7·25   1. 私は黒と赤が好きです。Watashi wa kuro to aka ga suki desu.
2. このドレスを着てみました。Kono doresu o kite mimashita.
3. このスカートをはいてみてください。Kono sukāto o haite mite kudasai.
4. セーターを買いすぎました。Sētā o kai-sugimashita.

7·26
  1. *We don't have a black one. We have a green one.*
  2. *Please try it on.*
  3. *But it's a little too small.*

7·27
  1. 上手に **jōzu ni** *skillfully*
  2. 静かに **shizuka ni** *quietly*
  3. 早く **hayaku** *early*
  4. まじめに **majime ni** *seriously*
  5. よく **yoku** *well*

7·28
  1. *You are a bit noisy. Could you study a bit more quietly, please?*
  2. *I cannot read it. Please write neatly. In addition, please write a bit bigger.*
  3. *The class is from 9 AM. Please come a bit earlier.*
  4. *I thought about it thoroughly. However, I plan not to do (take) this job.*
  5. *Could you be a bit more serious?*

7·29
  1. 静かにしてください。**Shizuka ni shite kudasai.**
  2. 部屋をきれいにしてください。**Heya o kirei ni shite kudasai.**
  3. あした早く来てください。**Ashita hayaku kite kudasai.**
  4. よく読んでください。**Yoku yonde kudasai.**

7·30
  1. どちらの方 **dochira no hō**   2. だれ **dare**   3. 何 **nani**   4. どれ **dore** (because it's a list of items)
  5. より **yori**   6. ほど **hodo**   7. と同じぐらい **to onaji gurai**

7·32
  1. 父は母ほどやさしくありません。**Chichi wa haha hodo yasashiku arimasen.**
  2. 中国語と日本語と，どちらの方が簡単ですか。**Chūgoku-go to Nihon-go to, dochira no hō ga kantan desu ka.**
  3. 車と飛行機と，どちらの方が安全ですか。**Kuruma to hikōki to, dochira no hō ga anzen desu ka.**
  4. カタカナはひらがなと同じぐらい簡単です。**Katakana wa hiragana to onaji gurai kantan desu.**
  5. 私は父より背が高いです。**Watashi wa chichi yori se ga takai desu.**

8   Making connections

8·1
  1. 行く **iku**   2. 飲んだ **nonda**   3. 食べなかった **tabenakatta**   4. 高かった **takakatta**
  5. きれいだった **kirei datta**   6. すしじゃなかった **sushi ja nakatta**

8·2
  1. 飲んでいた **nonde ita**   2. 飲めない **nomenai** (potential form)   3. 飲みたい **nomi-tai**
  4. 食べすぎた **tabe-sugita**   5. 着てみる **kite-miru**

8·3
  1. 私は日本語は簡単だと思います。**Watashi wa Nihon-go wa kantan da to omoimasu.**
  2. 私は漢字は書けないと思います。 **Watashi wa kanji wa kakenai to omoimasu.** (or 私は漢字が書けると思いません。**Watashi wa kanji ga kakeru to omoimasen.**)
  3. (私は)このセーターは大きすぎると思います。 **(Watashi wa) kono sētā wa ōki-sugiru to omoimasu.**
  4. (私は)あのレストランの食べ物はおいしかったと思います。 **(Watashi wa) ano resutoran no tabemono wa oishikatta to omoimasu.**
  5. 母はこのドレスは高すぎると思っています。 **Haha wa kono doresu wa takas-sugiru to omotte imasu.**

8·4
  1. 昨日来た男の人は日本人でした。**Kinō kita otoko no hito wa Nihon-jin deshita.** *The man who came (here) yesterday was Japanese.*
  2. 母が作ったてんぷらはおいしかったです。**Haha ga tsukutta tenpura wa oishikatta desu.** *The tempura my mother made was delicious.*
  3. 田中さんは昨日着ていた洋服を今日も着ています。**Tanaka-san wa kinō kite ita yōfuku o kyō mo kite imasu.** *Mr. Tanaka is wearing the clothes that he was wearing yesterday today also.*

8·5
  1. あそこでコーヒーを飲んでいる人は私の友達です。**Asoko de kōhī o nonde iru hito wa watashi no tomodachi desu.**
  2. 私が去年買った車はよくありません。**Watashi ga kyonen katta kuruma wa yoku arimasen.** (or . . . よくないです。. . . **yoku nai desu.**)
  3. あの犬は私が先週公園で見た犬です。**Ano inu wa watashi ga senshū kōen de mita inu desu.**

8·6
  1. 来月結婚するんです。**Raigetsu kekkon suru n desu.**
  2. お金がないんです。**O-kane ga nai n desu.** (Remember that ある **aru** is a slightly irregular **u** verb in that its **nai** form is just ない **nai**.)
  3. 会社を辞めたんです。**Kaisha o yameta n desu.**
  4. 私の父は韓国人なんです。**Watashi no chichi wa kankoku-jin na n desu.**

8·7
1. どうしてホテルをキャンセルしたんですか。**Dōshite hoteru o kyanseru shita n desu ka.** *Why did you cancel the hotel (reservation)?*
2. どうして会議に出ないんですか。**Dōshite kaigi ni denai n desu ka.** *Why are you not attending the conference?*
3. どうして山田さんの車を買わなかったんですか。**Dōshite Yamada-san no kuruma o kawanakatta n desu ka.** *Why didn't you buy Ms. Yamada's car?*
4. どうして韓国語を勉強しているんですか。**Dōshite Kankoku-go o benkyō shite iru n desu ka.** *Why are you studying Korean?*

8·8
1. 漢字が難しいからです。**Kanji ga muzukashii kara desu.** *It is because kanji is hard.*
2. お金がないからです。**O-kane ga nai kara desu.** *It is because I don't have money.*
3. とても高かったからです。**Totemo takakatta kara desu.** *It is because it was very expensive.*
4. あまりきれいじゃなかったからです。**Amari kirei ja nakatta kara desu.** *It is because it was not very pretty.*

8·10
1. 日本に行ったことがありますか。**Nihon ni itta koto ga arimasu ka.**
2. クレジットカードをなくしたことがありますか。**Kurejittokādo o nakushita koto ga arimasu ka.**
3. ヘリコプターに乗ったことがありますか。**Herikoputā ni notta koto ga arimasu ka.**
4. 宮崎駿のアニメを見たことがありますか。**Miyazaki Hayao no anime o mita koto ga arimasu ka.**

8·12
1. *Mike, have you been to Japan?*
2. *He was saying that it was very small.*
3. *I am thinking of staying there also. (I'd like to stay there also.)*

8·13
1. *It will probably be cloudy all day today.*
2. *It will probably rain tomorrow afternoon.*
3. *It will probably snow tomorrow evening.*
4. *It will probably be clear this weekend.*

8·14 1. 出 **de** 2. あり **ari** 3. 咳 **seki** 4. 痛い **itai**

8·15 1. yes 2. yes 3. no 4. possibly pneumonia

8·16
1. 昨日はテレビを見て宿題をして寝ました。**Kinō wa terebio mite shukudai o shite nemashita.** *I watched TV and did my homework yesterday.*
2. あしたは掃除をして買い物をして料理をします。**Ashita wa sōji o shite kaimono o shite ryōri o shimasu.** *I will go shopping and cook tomorrow.*
3. マイクさんは頭がよくて優しくてかっこいいです。**Maiku-san wa atama ga yokute yasashikute kakkoiidesu.** *Mike is smart, kind, and good-looking.*
4. メアリーさんはきれいで頭がいいです。**Mearī-san wa kirei de atama ga ii desu.** *Mary is pretty and smart.*
5. このレストランのすしは高くなくておいしいです。**Kono resutoran no sushi wa takaku nakute oishii desu.** *This restaurant's sushi is not expensive and delicious.*

8·17 1. じゃなくて **ja nakute** 2. あびないで **abinai de** 3. 来なくて **konakute**
4. すわないで **suwanai de** 5. おきられなくて **okirarenakute**

8·18
1. 私に聞いて買ってください。**Watashi ni kiite katte kudasai.**
2. 手を洗わないで食べないでください。**Te o arawanai de tabenai de kudasai.**
3. 頭が痛くて薬をのみました。**Atama ga itakute kusuri o nomimashita.**

8·19
1. おいしくありませんでしたが食べました。**Oishiku arimasendeshita ga tabemashita.**
2. 美香さんはきれいですが意地悪です。**Mika-san wa kirei desu ga ijiwaru desu.**
3. 日本語の試験を受けたいんですがどう思いますか。**Nihon-go no shiken o uketai n desu ga dō omoimasu ka.**
4. 3級は難しいですから4級を受けるつもりです。**San-kyū wa muzukashii desu kara yon-kyū o ukeru tsumori desu.**
5. あしたうちに田中さんが来ますが山田さんも来ませんか。**Ashita uchi ni Tanaka-san ga kimasu ga Yamada-san mo kimasen ka.**

9 Review exercises

9·5
1. 私は日本語の学生です。**Watashi wa Nihon-go no gakusei desu.** *I'm a student of Japanese.*
2. 私は中国からです。**Watashi wa Chūgoku kara desu.** *I'm from China.*
3. ケンさんは日本人じゃありません。**Ken-san wa Nihon-jin ja arimasen.** *Kin is not Japanese.*
4. あの人はだれですか。**Ano hito wa dare desu ka.** *Who is that person?*
5. あの人は谷さんの 妹さんです。**Ano hito wa Tani-san no imōto-san desu.** *That person is Mr. Tani's younger sister.*
   Or, 谷さんの 妹さんはあの人です。**Tani-san no imōto-san wa ano hito desu.** *Mr. Tani's younger sister is that person.*

9·6	パリ **Pari** *Paris*
	ボストン **Bosuton** *Boston*
	トロント **Toronto** *Toronto*
	ロンドン **Rondon** *London*
	ローマ **Rōma** *Rome*

9·7
1. あの **ano**
2. あの人 **Ano hito**
3. この **Kono**
4. それ **Sore**
5. これ **Kore**

9·8
1. はじめまして。**Hajimemashite.**
2. どうもありがとうございます。**Dōmo arigatō gozaimasu.**
3. すみません。**Sumimasen.**
4. おはようございます。**Ohayō gozaimasu.**

9·9
1. さんびゃくどる **sanbyaku-doru**
2. せんえん **sen-en**
3. ぜろさん ろくななよんに いちごはちさん **zero san - roku nana yon ni - ichi go hachi san**
4. にじゅうさんさい **nijūsan-sai**
5. しちがつ にじゅういちにち **shichi-gatsu nijū-ichi-nichi**
6. ごご よじ **gogo yo-ji**
7. ごぜん ごじ じゅうごふん **gozen go-ji jūgo-fun**
8. にせんじゅうはちねん **nisenjūhachi-nen**
9. いつつ **itsu-tsu**

9·10　　1. Wednesday　　2. Tuesday　　3. Friday　　4. Saturday　　5. Monday

9·12
1. あのカメラはいくらですか。**Ano kamera wa ikura desu ka.**
2. あのカメラとこのスキャナーをください。**Ano kamera to kono sukyanā o kudasai.**
3. 切手を3枚ください。**Kitte o san-mai kudasai.**
4. ねこが2匹います。**Neko ga ni-hiki imasu.**
5. 本が3冊あります。**Hon ga san-satsu arimasu.**

9·13　　1. a　　2. e　　3. c　　4. b　　5. d

9·14
1. 行きます **ikimasu**
2. 来ます **kimasu**
3. 帰ります **kaerimasu**
4. 歩きます **arukimasu**
5. 買います **kaimasu**
6. 待ちます **machimasu**
7. 食べます **tabemasu**
8. 泳ぎます **oyogimasu**
9. します **shimasu**

9·15
1. 今日はスーパーに行きます。**Kyō wa sūpā ni ikimasu.**
2. 明日はどこにも行きません。**Ashita wa doko ni mo ikimasen.**
3. 明日どこかに行きますか。**Ashita wa doko-ka ni ikimasu ka.**
4. 今日はどこに行きますか。**Kyō wa doko ni ikimasu ka.**

9·16
1. で **de**
2. に **ni**
3. 行きます **ikimasu**
4. 行きません **ikimasen**
5. 帰ります **kaerimasu**
6. 見 **mi**
7. 歩いて **aruite**

9·17
1. うたわない **utawanai**
2. 作らない **tsukuranai**
3. 切らない **kiranai**
4. 着ない **kinai**
5. 寝ない **nenai**
6. 起きない **okinai**
7. 来ない **konai**
8. しない **shinai**

9·18
1. 買って katte
2. 読んで yonde
3. 話して hanashite

9·19
1. 書ける kakeru
2. 飛べる toberu
3. 泳げる oyogeru

9·20
1. でも Demo
2. を o
3. が ga
4. で de
5. で de
6. ねない nenai
7. はなせ hanase
8. すわないで suwanaide
9. 来ていません kite imasen
10. と to

9·21
1. d   2. e   3. c   4. b   5. a

9·22
1. ペンはかばんの中にあります。
   Pen wa kaban no naka ni arimasu.
2. 名古屋は東京と大阪の間にあります。
   Nagoya wa Tōkyō to Ōsaka no aida ni arimasu.

9·23
1. あります arimasu
2. います imasu
3. いらっしゃいます irasshaimasu
4. います imasu
5. あります arimasu
6. あります arimasu
7. あります arimasu
8. あります arimasu

9·24
1. それから Sorekara
2. そうすると Sōsuruto
3. ですから Desukara
   Translation: *Please go straight on this street.*
   Then, turn left at the seventh intersection.
   Then, you'll see my company on your right.
   There is a bus stop in front of my company.
   So, you can also take a bus to go there.

9·25
1. g   2. h   3. a   4. f   5. e   6. d
7. c   8. b

9·26
1. はいて haite
2. して shite
3. 高くありません takaku arimasen
4. と to
5. 寒かった samukatta

9·27
1. より yori
2. どんな donna
3. どうして dōshite
4. して shite
5. や ya

9·28
1. 私はマンガが大好きです。
   それで, マンガを読みすぎました。
   Watashi wa manga ga dai-suki desu.
   Sorede, manga o yomi-sugimashita.
2. 私はすしが好きです。
   でも, すしは高すぎます。
   Watashi wa sushi ga suki desu.
   Demo, sushi wa taka-sugimasu.
3. 私はこのドレスを着てみました。
   でも, 好きじゃありませんでした。
   それに, 高すぎました。
   Watashi wa kono doresu o kite mimashita.
   Demo, suki ja arimasendeshita.
   Soreni, taka-sugimashita.
4. 私は掃除をするのが好きです。
   昨日はキッチンをきれいにしました。
   Watashi wa sōji o suru no ga suki desu.
   Kinō wa kitchin o kirei ni shimashita.

9·29
1. c   2. e   3. a   4. d   5. b

9·30
1. b   2. d   3. a   4. e   5. c

9·31
1. 数学は簡単だと思います。
   Sūgaku wa kantan da to omoimasu.
2. 飲みすぎたかもしれません。
   Nomi-sugita-kamoshiremasen.
3. 日曜日は雪がふるでしょう。
   Nichiyōbi wa yuki ga furu-deshō.
4. 富士山を見たことがありますか。
   Fuji-san o mita koto ga arimasu ka.
5. 来月結婚するんです。
   Raigetsu kekkon suru n desu.

9·32
1. 高かったですが, よかったです。
   Takakatta desu ga, yokatta desu.
2. これは日本で買ったんですが, とても便利ですよ。
   Kore wa Nihon de katta n desu ga, totemo benri desu yo.
3. 朝ごはんを食べないでクラスに行きましたから, 今おなかがすいています。
   Asa-gohan o tabenai de kurasu ni ikimashita kara, ima onaka ga suite imasu.